FIVE WAYS TO COOK ASPARAGUS

FIVE WAYS TO COOK ASPARAGUS

(AND OTHER RECIPES)

The Art and Practice of Making Dinner

PETER MILLER

Photographs by Hirsheimer & Hamilton

Illustrations by Colleen Miller

ABRAMS / NEW YORK

CONTENTS

PREFACE
Heading Home

We are going to eat at home. There may be no time to shop. You may not have thought about what to make. There may be parts and pieces, but no plan for how to use them.

This is a cookbook for workdays. It offers ideas for getting dinner started, getting it done that evening, and keeping it going day after day.

I cook seven days a week and need a cookbook that can handle that kind of schedule. I need to be able to improvise and make do, and at the end of the day, I need to be pleased with the meal. And pleased to cook it.

INTRODUCTION
Making Dinner

This is a book about making dinner—about making it in real time and preparing it under real conditions. The meals are obviously important, but often there is no time to do careful shopping, planning, or preparation. There may only be time to get the meal ready.

I own a bookshop near the Pike Place Market in Seattle, and depending on the season, the days can begin early and they can go a little late. Often, I walk through the market on my way home; just as often, the purveyors are already packing up when I get there. I missed them in the morning, and I missed them at night. It is lovely to have an afternoon to talk to the butcher and to go over what is in and what is out with the fruit and vegetable people. But it is not always possible. Sometimes, you must simply cook and make do. Sometimes, there are no roasts, fish, or chicken at the ready, but there is still a dinner to be constructed.

No matter how busy or crisscrossed your day has been, there are ways to eat well. A good soup may handle the task on nights that only need a light meal. With a little care and attention, asparagus and rice can ably sit in as a weekday supper. A plate of pasta, with a few details, may seem a quiet feast. The hard part is recognizing the possibilities on hand.

My staff and I prepare lunch every day at our bookshop. My first cookbook, *Lunch at the Shop*, distilled our experience into a manual, detailing how anyone can eat lunch well, even during busy workdays. But now I want to focus on dinner, at the end of whatever kind of day you might have had.

A cookbook's job is to cook. That is what *Five Ways to Cook Asparagus* means to do—to help you get meals ready by offering inspiration, advice on preparation, and encouragement to enjoy the process and the meals.

Where to Start?

For most days it is an honor to do the cooking—to be the cook. There are the obvious difficulties of supplies and provisions, of new seasons and new products, of having the time and having the will. Often, the true difficulty is the sense of what would work, what would be best, what would be appropriate, and what we should have.

It is the task of where to begin. One thing may lead to another, but first you need some inspiration. On some days, it might be chicken or fish. On others,

1 bag arugula
1 bunch asparagus ~~...~~

~~...~~
~~COFFEE BEANS~~
~~...~~
~~PEPPER...~~

~~PEPPE~~

3 ripe pears
1/2 c. walnuts

1 bag. baby arugula
1 lb. FETA
1 lb. THYME
~~1 CAN OLIVE OIL~~
~~PAPA~~
~~TOMATO~~
~~ADZ~~
~~SPANISH~~ HAM PROSCIUTTO
~~SAUSAGE~~ JAMON LUGANEGA
~~...~~

WATER ~~MILK~~

TURKISH
RED PEPPER
FLAKES
MILK.

1/2 lb. fresh favas in their pods
~~1/4 lb.~~ JAMON SERANO - thinly sliced
~~1/2~~ pancetta
2 lamb thighs - TOP ROUND
~~1 oregano~~
1 can San Marzano pomodori pelati
1 lbs. Monkfish, blue membrane removed

a soup or a salad. You need the start of a trail, a place to begin, and then the details can unfold and make some sense.

For me, the entry point is rarely a big bird or a long steak and more often a detail—a tomato coming into season, a wild mushroom, chives, basil, fresh corn, a variety of lentil I have not tried, or even a new source for dried beans. A single ingredient can provide a spark of inspiration, and then cooking seems to lose much of its burden. It gathers momentum. To get a meal prepared, you must work with ingredients, time, and inspiration. They are your terms and, with some luck and care, your most crucial allies.

Cooking by Fives

I do not stack recipes on end, like dominoes, to take me through the week and weekend—that, to me, would be an assignment. Instead, I begin with some questions: *What can I get, where are we, what is the season, what is the weather, what is the mood? How much time will I have to cook, to shop? What would please me, and what will please the people for whom I am cooking?*

And then I can start to figure it out. It may be a seasonal detail—spinach, for example, that I rarely think about except in the spring, when it is so subtle and fresh that it can be added to nearly everything. It may be the weather—the comfort and endurance on a cold day of cannellini and cranberry beans, which can make a meal by themselves or accommodate multiple variations. It may be convenience—I know a prepared bolognese sauce can be added to just about everything and so will make my cooking half the task. That can be a great help during busy weeks.

Help may come from many directions. I know that from a good roasted chicken, two or even three wonderful meals will directly emerge—a chicken and leek soup, a creamy risotto, and a roast chicken panzanella, for instance—and there are even a couple of lunches to be pulled from it.

I know that shellfish are at their best in the winter, that asparagus should be played all spring, that true wild mushrooms can lift one's spirit and one's pasta, that fresh tomatoes should be celebrated every day they are available, that toasting day-old bread can carry an entire meal, that a good cookbook can be more important for its optimism than its recipes, that parsley is as obvious as a cotton pillowcase, that good food is healthier than bad food.

Five Ways to Cook Asparagus celebrates this kind of knowledge: the importance of the details, and how to best use particular ingredients. Organized around the number five, this book is inspired by a hypothetical five-day work-week. The number five is our boundary, offering a plan to make the best use of your time, your materials, and your interest in good and healthy food. There are many possible directions, but our map begins from five points.

The number five is a solution. You have workdays to plan for and, typically, little time to do the planning. The best help, in my experience, is to have a few quick, tried-and-tested paths—ways that you can react to both the food you might have on hand and the food that has suddenly come into season. Once you get the optimism of a few ideas, the rollout of each meal is less imposing. It is a task of starting out as much as it is a task of cooking.

The intent of focusing on certain foods—whether asparagus or broccoli, cauliflower or lentils, rice or beans—is to make each one fundamentally clear and to bring each one alive, strengthened with the details of its history and its natural gifts. The set of foods in the pages to follow was carefully selected. They are the important items to have in your larder—delicious and versatile ingredients with which to build a relationship. They make a powerful, adaptable arsenal.

I am not trying to make anything simpler. I am trying to make it possible and more of a pleasure. If you can make this recipe, then you can make another, and if you can do that, then ten more things will come to mind.

Today's Food Supply

I was not raised with five ways to cook asparagus or cauliflower. Meals were a simpler regimen than that, constructed of a protein, potato, and vegetable, and, in the warmer months, a salad. We never thought to experiment with the techniques of Vietnam or the Middle East, or those of Mexico or Peru—to practice the subtleties of Spanish cuisine or the long knowledge of Italy. There were fewer alternatives and certainly fewer supplies. It was a narrower map.

But the doors to cooking, the details to nearly every food culture on this earth, are near to fully open now. And their influence will only broaden. We have the knowledge of and interest in making meals that would not even have been considered twenty years ago. The ingredients have become more specific and more accurate. The products have, in many cases, been rescued from neglect and commodity.

It is a live condition, your food supply, and the more you have a good sense of it, the better your cooking will be, and the more your meals will reflect your actual place and time. Ingredients, and knowing which are best and available, are true and natural guides to being a good cook.

I can now buy lovely dried beans and lentils and rice and know the dates and origin of each one of them. I can source the meats and chicken and fish, choosing them as they are best available. My grocer is pleased to say that the asparagus is a good month away from being released or that the peas are gone for the season. My baker is looking for better wheat, and the yogurt maker is using better milk. My son chides me that I have only started to learn about quinoa.

The flood of information about food has contributed a superb complexity to the standards of cooking, but the need for selection and pattern is more apparent than ever. A visual display of sixteen different carrot dishes that one can make is a fine online distraction, but it does not help me get a meal ready. For that, I need a more rigorous focus that cuts through the clutter and assembles the best available cast. And that is where the number five comes in—a collection of five simple, appealing ways to handle the season's or your larder's bounty (or lack thereof).

There seems to be less time to shop, and less time to cook, and yet time spent eating together seems more important than ever. I may cook a dinner with only one or two fresh ingredients and give them particular attention, and I must have the confidence that it will be enough.

Beyond the Recipe

I have often read and tried a new recipe that, for me, had no context. I would follow it, even as an acolyte, but I was only cooking by its numbers. It was a new dance step or, in some cases, almost a new magic trick and an adventure.

Until I weaned myself from the exact written recipe, until it became, in whatever form, part of all I know and sense about food—until then, it sat in a particular isolation. If I signed on to the recipe as is, I curiously signed out of my own talents and intuitions and reactions. I was a good soldier, but not a very good cook and, in a way, not myself.

You can sense the blood of a recipe. It has a pulse, however faint or furious. And it has crucial intersections, moments when it gives specific direction, where you must go, how you must get there, and how quickly. It is in those details that you must find and take what you can from a recipe. And make it part of your own strength. You may try to memorize the details, but you must actually internalize them, understand them, and make them a part of what you know about cooking. You can always go back to it for specifics, but make certain to take from it some sense of why it works and why you danced with it.

With *Five Ways to Cook Asparagus*, there are, of course, recipes, but I have kept them in the simplest formats possible. My favorite ways of grilling asparagus and cooking rice do not require elaborate techniques, after all. These fundamental methods, focused on a limited set of ingredients, are intended to help expand your knowledge of some versatile foods and hone your skills in preparing them.

Making a recipe is a little like hiking a new trail. At first, you are tiptoeing and tentative, unsure of lengths and time and dangers. But as you return, you get better and better at it and you begin to know it, to see its point, to see its structure, and finally, to see where it is taking you. By then, you are no longer looking at your steps, you have all your wits back, and you are already making adjustments. The trail is in your muscle memory.

If you do make your own dinners, if you practice it, get good at it, and start to cook intuitively, if you start to believe it, and shop for it, and cook at night for it, if you look it right in the eye and make sense of it, then you will have something. You will be a partner to seasons and food culture, a quiet director of smells and colors, habits, and tastes, a part of history and invention.

At its best, you are cooking to use the past, to sustain the present, and to account for the future. At its most basic, you are using the foods that need to be used, you are keeping a close eye on the day and your guests, and you will have a future meal nearly ready, or at least half prepped—all in spite of your hectic schedule. And in any case, do not worry. You will have lots of help along the way . . . the people on this trail love to cook.

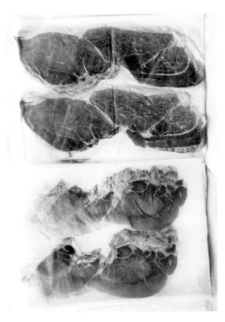

LARDER

Five Types of Foods to Keep in Stock

We start in the belly of your kitchen. Your larder is where meals are born. You must protect it, keep it clean and fresh and visible, know its dates and shortages and prospects. Some ingredients will change with each season, often nearly disappearing at times, but it is the proper larder that will give you confidence, the knowledge that you are always ready and able to cook.

In the pages to follow, five basic categories of foods that are handy to keep in your kitchen are listed—dairy products, greens, liquids like olive oils and vinegars, breads, and fruits, with five essential representatives of each category explained. Advice on sourcing is given, and a recipe that allows each essential ingredient to shine is provided.

Each item in the larder has separate needs—some will be fine with little attention and some will need daily attention; some should be kept on hand every day of the week and some may appear in your kitchen every few days. It is a kind of barnyard, but it is the barnyard that you must cook from, and the barnyard that will be the most help with the alchemy of making meals.

THE FIVE GREENS

Parsley / Arugula / Butter Lettuce /
Cilantro / Swiss Chard

PARSLEY

It gets faint credit, but parsley is a shy beacon in a kitchen and a specific light in any presentation. It is available every day of the year, but it is at its brightest when the sun and the spring have returned.

There are two kinds of parsley—the flat-leafed version, often called Italian parsley, and the curly-leafed variety. I use both of them, but I use flat-leaf parsley most of the time. It is less bitter and has a more interesting texture when it is chopped. Flat-leaf parsley is part of the celery family, and its leaves can appear near identical to those of celery. You can only distinguish them by smell or taste.

I will use the curly-leafed variety if there is no other choice or in dishes that might be reused several times, like a couscous or quinoa, as the curly variety stays wonderfully crisp and green.

The difficulty of parsley is that it can feel more like a logo or a signature than an actual food. It seems an obligation, a flourish added at the end. But give it more credit. Many times, it will be the very difference to a dish. It is the literal signal of freshness and immediacy, of care and attention and pace. It is the taste of fresh greens, it is the color of new growth, and it is the texture of actual plant and leaf.

You must take some care when you buy it. For one thing, it is often as well-handled as a dollar bill. Each customer seems to pick all the bunches up, looking for the best one or the largest one. When you get home, take the elastic or twist tie off, rinse the parsley under cool running water, then plunge it into a big bowl of fresh cold water. Let it rest for a few minutes in the bowl, then lift it out and shake it to get the loose water off. (If the water left in the bowl is particularly dirty or cloudy, soak the parsley again in fresh water. There may have been strong rains or some bacteria.)

Once you have shaken the parsley bunch well, set it in an upright plastic container (a large yogurt container works well) or in a zip-top bag, stems down. If they are too long, trim them to fit. Stored in the refrigerator, it should keep that way for at least a week. If you plan to use it in a day or two, then simply keep it on the counter in a large glass with a couple of inches of fresh water in the bottom. Change the water every morning. Once I start to cook, I always chop the parsley first.

Pick the leaves off, toss the stems into any stock you might have on the side, and put the chopped parsley into a clean, small bowl. I might chop some of the parsley with a pinch of sea salt and then use that on fish or chicken—or chop it with some thin slices of garlic. You can then add it to the coating of a steak or the sautéing of vegetables or mushrooms.

In the colder months, when you are slow-cooking short ribs and shanks and stews, you can take the parsley even further, adding not only finely chopped garlic but also very thin slivers of lemon peel to create a gremolata. Mince the lemon, garlic, and parsley together, adding a little salt for grip, and sprinkle that over the final dish, adding the brightness of their taste to the denseness of the slow-cooked meat.

But in basic terms, I simply chop the parsley and set it nearby. And I do that first so the parsley will only have its specific taste, rather than others from the cutting board. I will guess how much parsley I might need, and if there is any leftover, I add it to anything that is also leftover. It is the start of my cooking and the very end of my cooking.

Parsley Sauce

Leaves from 1 bunch
parsley, chopped

Flaky sea salt

¼ to ½ cup (60 to
120 ml) extra-virgin
olive oil

MAKES 1 CUP (240 ML)

Sometimes, when it is most abundant and flavorful, I will make a quick sauce of chopped parsley, stirring the ingredients together with a fork. You can do this in a food processor, but it is so simple and even rhythmic to blend the sauce with a good dinner fork, rolling it over and over, tasting it for salt and the relation of oil and parsley. When you get it to just the right proportion, when you can dip a piece of bread into the sauce and be pleased, then it is ready. Use the sauce to enliven grilled sandwiches, to spoon over sliced meats or pieces of fish, to detail a plate of roasted vegetables, to add complexity to yogurt and hummus. Or simply grill or broil leftover breads and pitas and pieces of pizza and finish them with this lovely sauce.

In a medium glass bowl, stir together the parsley and some salt. While stirring, slowly add the olive oil. Salt will not dissolve in olive oil, but it needs to be evenly distributed. Taste as you go. You can use a food processor, but pulse just once or twice to barely mix. Store the sauce in a jar or airtight container—it should keep for 3 to 4 days in the refrigerator.

ARUGULA

You can get tired of hearing about arugula. It was one of the first greens to sashay around, acting like it was better than the hardworking Bibb and romaine and butter lettuces. The truth is, it is often quite remarkable—not all of the time, but often enough that you should always be ready when it is at its best.

Learn what it looks like when it is at its peak. The leaves are a middle green, neither pale nor dark. There is no mottling. The stems are unbroken. As it ages, the leaves get oversized and hardened, and you must pick off most of the stem.

Once the outdoor field crop is done, then you must rely on the greenhouse arugula, which is typically sold in clear plastic boxes. It is perfectly good—all the leaves are small and the same size and it is available all year long. It is, in effect, the cyborg of arugula, a technological miracle, but, as they say, not great company on long train rides. I am glad to have it in December, when little else is available, but it is not subtle enough then to be a salad all by itself. It is best used as an accessory.

But in the start of spring or the brace of fall, the arugula is simply a glory. The leaves and stems are a perfect match. The taste has a slight sweetness, and it will jump right up to lemon juice and fresh black pepper, to good salt and true vinegar, to olive oils, and even anchovies, to yogurt, and to fresh Parmesan.

When it is just right—fresh and young and bountiful—then I will use it in everything. I will toss it raw into soups just before serving. I will make a bed of it and lay grilled fish or steaks right on top. I will layer every plate with it and then put the roasted beets, potatoes, asparagus, or broccoli onto it. And I will make this salad.

But-a-Minute Arugula Salad

Juice of 1 lemon

1 tablespoon white
    wine vinegar

Sea salt

1 teaspoon fresh
    Tellicherry
    peppercorns

¼ cup (60 ml) extra-
    virgin olive oil

1 pound (455 g) fresh
    arugula

2 tablespoons freshly
    grated Parmigiano-
    Reggiano cheese

4 slices country bread,
    grilled (optional)

1 garlic clove (optional)

SERVES 4

This salad takes but a moment. You must have good greens, a fresh lemon, extra-virgin olive oil, and very good peppercorns to make it work properly.

In a large stainless-steel bowl, whisk together the lemon juice, vinegar, and 1 teaspoon of salt. The salt will, in a minute, dissolve. If you have a good adjustable pepper grinder, set it on its coarsest grind and give four turns of the grinder into the mix. If you do not have such a grinder, coarsely crack the peppercorns by hand and scrape the pieces into the bowl. Stir to combine. While stirring, slowly add the olive oil. Taste and adjust the seasoning. If the peppercorns are good, you will taste their quick, dark heat. Adjust the salt, if need be.

Lay the greens on top of the dressing. Sprinkle a little salt over them and then, with tongs or salad servers, toss the greens over a couple of times through the dressing in the bowl, quickly and lightly. Lightly set the greens on salad plates. There should be some dressing remaining in the bowl. The leaves should not be drowning in the dressing and should stand up a little on the plates. If they lay flat like wet leaves, something got too wet.

Crack more pepper on top and sprinkle the cheese around. If you grilled some bread, rub the grilled side with a little garlic and pour a thin drizzle of the leftover salad dressing across the face of the bread. Then cut the bread into a couple of strips and serve them alongside the salad.

BUTTER LETTUCE

There are at least three varieties of butter lettuce, more accurately but less prosaically named butterhead lettuce, and they all share the quality of loose and tender leaves. There is Boston, Bibb, and red leaf. Their tastes are similar and always pleasant, if not almost sweet.

Boston lettuce is slightly larger and less distinct in its leaf shape. Bibb is the most elegant in terms of size and appearance, and red leaf is the most sprawling of the bunch and seems the most economic, for the leaves can grow to twice the size of a Bibb. The butter lettuce group is so-called because their leaves are tender.

Any of the three can serve perfectly as the host of a salad, receiving all manner of contributions from other, more particular greens such as mesclun and arugula.

In contrast to other, more sturdy lettuce types, a romaine for example, the butter lettuce must be handled with certain care. The leaves must be soaked in cold water, and then rinsed gently as if they were a wide glove. They must then be drained in a large kitchen colander, and dried further in a large kitchen towel or a spinner.

If you take care in their washing and store them in perforated bags in the refrigerator, the leaves will keep perfectly for two to three days. They simply need a little personal attention. At their best, butter lettuces are the most elegant main characters in a salad or sandwich or the most memorable supporting roles beneath a main course.

Butter Lettuce Salad, Alone

1 teaspoon Dijon
mustard

1 tablespoon red wine
vinegar

Sea salt

3 tablespoons extra-
virgin olive oil

1 head butter lettuce,
soaked, rinsed, and
dried

1 tablespoon chopped
fresh chives

1 tablespoon freshly
grated Parmigiano-
Reggiano cheese

Fresh ground black
pepper

SERVES 4

This is a good way to learn why people love butter lettuce. It is a slight indulgence to only use butter lettuce.

In a small bowl, mix the mustard, vinegar, and some salt, and then slowly whisk in the olive oil.

Tear the lettuce leaves at least in half, but gently, and drop them into a cold salad bowl.

Pour the dressing over the greens and toss them several times to coat. Then add the chives, toss, add the cheese, and toss again. Finish with salt and pepper.

CILANTRO

I have said it before: If you want to use and understand cilantro, then use it in abundance. Once, I would chop six to eight leaves to add to rice. Now, I will chop two or three whole bunches of cilantro, stems and leaves together, by hand or in a food processor—several cups of chopped cilantro, all told—and add it to the rice.

It has its particulars: It is not easily chopped because it never gets as dry as flat-leaf parsley, for example. You must store it with some attention. It does not like moisture. In its DNA heart, it is a southern hemisphere herb.

Cilantro is the Spanish word for "coriander"and refers to the stem and leaves of the coriander plant. The seed of cilantro is called coriander. Typically, the seeds are dried and then reheated or at least mortared to a powder as a crucial spice in Middle Eastern, Indian, and Asian cuisines. The unripe coriander seed is green and rarely available. If you can get some, they are the child of cilantro and coriander in flavor, and are wonderful in sauces or dressings.

Cilantro is a true ally to parsley. They are often chopped and added together—the slight lemon flavor of the cilantro alongside the very green and fresh taste of the parsley. Make a salsa verde of them and you will see how wonderful they are together.

Salsa Verde

1 cup (50 g) chopped
fresh flat-leaf parsley

1 cup (40 g) chopped
fresh cilantro

1 teaspoon grated
lemon zest

Juice of 1 lemon

1 garlic clove, finely
chopped

1 teaspoon sea salt

1 tablespoon capers,
rinsed

½ cup (120 ml) extra-
virgin olive oil

MAKES 1 CUP (240 ML)

Use this salsa verde on meats and meatballs, on chicken and fish, on grilled vegetables, on lentils and beans, on soups and salads. Keep it in an airtight container in the fridge, but let it come to room temperature before using. If need be, you can add a little more olive oil to thin it.

In a stainless-steel bowl, stir together all the ingredients except the olive oil. While whisking, slowly add the olive oil. Store in an airtight container—it will keep in the refrigerator for 3 to 4 days.

SWISS CHARD

I would not have made much room for Swiss chard had it not insistently shown up in my CSA-delivered vegetables. Swiss chard is a hearty one, an athlete of the greens, and it is much easier to grow than spinach and just as nutritious. It is a bit like beet greens and rhubarb—you simply need to make a little room for them in your planning.

Preparing Swiss chard is in truth quite straightforward. When it is very young, you can eat all of the leaf. Simply trim off the hard bottom stem, wash the chard very well, and add it, still wet, to a pan to blanch. Add some salt and cook it, covered, for 6 to 8 minutes or so, until it has softened. Then drain the greens, pushing the water out of them. Then they are ready to serve, and need only a little bit of red wine vinegar or lemon, olive oil, and salt and pepper.

After blanching the leaves, you can also sauté them. Do drain the water out (but do not squeeze them like a sponge—they bruise) and then lightly cut the greens into smaller pieces. Heat some olive oil in a sauté pan, add some chopped garlic and a pinch of hot red pepper flakes, and when you smell the garlic, add the greens and stir to mix. Let them sauté for 2 minutes, add some salt and pepper, and they are ready.

If the Swiss chard is more mature, as is often the case, then separate the leaves from the tough stalk and deal with the leaves and stems separately. Cook the leaves as above. For the stalks, cut them into shorter lengths, and put them into a pot of salted boiling water for 18 to 20 minutes, until they are soft. Drain the stalks and use them as you will the leaves—sautéed, dressed, or as additions to soups.

When you get Swiss chard, think of making soup. It is brilliant in soup, especially minestrones and bean soups that have the strength and volume to take up the chard. You can add the uncooked stems and greens at the start of a soup, or blanch them and add them later.

Swiss Chard and a Few White Beans

¼ cup (60 ml) extra-
virgin olive oil, plus
more as needed

2 garlic cloves, finely
chopped

I pound (455 g) fresh
Swiss chard, soaked,
rinsed well, and
chopped into 2-inch
(5-cm) pieces

Sea salt and fresh
ground black pepper

¼ cup (40 g) cooked
cannellini beans

SERVES 3 TO 4

**If you have some fresh Swiss chard and want a quick sampler
as an appetizer, try it with some cooked cannellini beans. Swiss
chard loves being with beans.**

Choose a sauté pan that can hold the Swiss chard and heat it over
medium heat. Add the olive oil and the garlic and, moments later,
the Swiss chard. (If the chard is mature and stiff, then cover the
pan to get more heat to it. If the chard is young, you can cook it
uncovered.) Add some salt and ground pepper and stir it all to mix.

The chard should be ready in 6 to 8 minutes. Taste a piece, and if it
is tender, add the cannellini beans. Stir well, to combine the beans
into the greens. When the beans are heated through, serve in a
warm bowl with extra olive oil and more grinds of black pepper.

THE FIVE LIQUIDS
Olive Oil / Vinegars / Stock /

Water / Alcohol

OLIVE OIL

It is not a simple matter to choose your olive oil. There are too many factors, too many places to hide (the packaging often being better than the oil), and too many customers. It was once, even ten years ago, a quite simple matter to find a good olive oil and, when you felt wealthy or worthy, a very good olive oil. But the customers for olive oil have multiplied tenfold: People have learned to love its taste, to trust its nature, to believe in its quietly mythic assets. Climates have become more fragile, entire seasons have been lost to uncommon droughts and rains, and the sheer pressure of modernism has threatened the supply—and, of course, broadened the attempts to grow olives wherever it might be possible.

You must now be more cautious. Many olive oils are a blend, which is not in itself a terrible matter, but they are often concealing a weakness of quality. For my part, I simply want an honest olive oil. I do not want it to be deceitful regarding its origin or its value. I want its taste to be authentic, and I want its provenance to be accurate.

For my everyday olive oil, I use Partanna, a Sicilian extra-virgin oil, and have since it was recommended to me ten years ago. We use it at the shop as well, for cooking and for dressings. For a fancier oil, I asked DeLaurenti's, our wonderful Italian market, for their favorite, and they all agreed on Poggio la Noce, a Tuscan all-natural olive oil. Once you have tasted a fine Tuscan oil, with all its flavors and hints of elegance, then that becomes its own standard. The trick is to find a true version—Poggio la Noce is precisely that.

You must use and trust your olive oil suppliers. It is their reputation that is being wagered, so they should be able to help. They will know which oils have the highest regard—which oils have quietly emerged and been praised.

It is difficult to simply trust your taste. Anyone can make olive oil taste greener or subtly herbal. You must start first with the designation extra virgin, for that will eliminate the largest percentage of fraud. To be extra virgin, the olive oil must have been extracted in the least manipulative, most fundamental manner possible—a cold process of mechanical crushing. The oil is then measured for its acidity (anything above 1 percent acidity and the oil cannot be labeled "extra virgin").

It is an awkward term in English and that does not help its credibility or reputation. I have often heard people say olive oil is olive oil, as water is water, but that is not true, for either of them.

You can make tomato sauce with six different olive oils and achieve six different sauces. It is most important that you learn the different results. Some of them you will quietly cherish, some you will simply forget, and some you will be careful to never use again. Olive oil has a way of sitting within your memory.

When you have found an oil you like, other factors become important. The villains to olive oil are heat and light and air, and obviously they are difficult to avoid. You cannot leave the oil above the stove or alongside the stove, except for the time you are making a meal. You cannot let it sit luxuriantly on the windowsill. You cannot leave it for months in the oil can from Parma.

It is fragile. Keep it cool and in the dark. Keep it tightly sealed and decant only what you will use in a day or two. Check its date before you buy the oil. It should ideally be no more than a year old. And, once you open the container, then a new clock begins to tick, for you must then use it within months, not years. By taking care of your olive oil, by accepting its fragility, you will better understand its cost and better appreciate its use.

The Simplest Dressed Salad

1 teaspoon sea salt

3 cups (120 to 165 g)
fresh greens, washed
and spun dry

¼ cup (60 ml) extra-
virgin olive oil

1 tablespoon red or
white wine vinegar

Fresh cracked black
pepper

SERVES 4 TO 6

Sometimes to really appreciate the rich taste of a good olive oil you just need to make a basic salad. The vinegar, a basic red or white wine variety, is held back until the end. Use the largest bowl that you can find when you are tossing a salad—better it seems a little lonely in the bowl than that it be spilling out. If the greens are fresh, washed and dried, the oil fresh as well, if you used enough salt that it can just be tasted, if there was room to toss the greens and not simply to roll them over, if the vinegar is bright and the cracked pepper as well, then you will think this salad is all that a salad need be.

I realize that it involves a lot of "ifs," but that is the nature of this salad. It is not trying to hide anything. It is a show of elegance, confidence, and immediacy. Done.

Salt the greens first, tossing them two or three times in a large bowl, then add the olive oil and toss again to coat the leaves. Add the vinegar at the very finish and toss quickly to mix. Then crack some pepper over it all and the salad is ready.

VINEGARS

Unlike olive oil, vinegar can be stored for longer periods. It is threatened more by evaporation than time, so keep it in an airtight container and it should be fine.

It is a particular taste, and in truth, each person seems to have their own relation to the taste. When I make a salad dressing to serve to others, the basic relation of olive oil to vinegar is 3 parts oil to 1 part vinegar. For myself, I prefer 4 parts olive oil, but only if I know the olive oil is pretty good and that it has an agreeable taste. For proportions, use a shot glass or similar small glass. It is hard to be very accurate measuring ¼ cup (60 ml) of olive oil in a measuring cup, and I lose patience using tablespoons.

If I am making a dressing for a salad that has very frail greens, I might add a drop more vinegar, as a kind of sparkle. The same is true of tomatoes—if I am serving a plate of sliced fresh tomatoes, I will sprinkle the slightest touch of vinegar across the surface.

I typically use red or white vinegar, but of course, you can use balsamic vinegar. It is a brilliant creation, an Italian third cousin to Bénédictine liqueurs. At its truest, balsamic vinegar is viscous and almost coldly molten, a furtive creation kept back for twelve years before it is even allowed in the kitchen. There are many, many pretenders now—and there are even sauces, to be squeezed from tubes—as if the acid and the sweet were simply something to be assembled from parts.

A true balsamic vinegar should be added only in drops, near the end of tossing the greens. It is not a smear, and it seems a shame to puddle it below olive oil for dipping into. I think of it as a dropper, a tincture, of a particular sweetness. I have a near full jar that was a gift and I feel that it will last me forever.

A True Vinaigrette

1 tablespoon red or
white wine vinegar

1 teaspoon sea salt

¼ cup (60 ml) extra-
virgin olive oil

Fresh cracked black
pepper

MAKES 5 TABLESPOONS (75 ML)

This salad dressing, one of my favorites, a true vinaigrette, begins with the vinegar, which is its base. Use a white or a red vinegar, but make certain that it is a quality brand. The vinaigrette will keep well in a sealed jar for a couple of weeks. I typically refrigerate it, but if you do, it must come to room temperature before it will regain its taste. Then simply shake it well to mix.

Put the vinegar in a small bowl and sprinkle the salt over it. Let it sit for a minute—the salt will dissolve in the vinegar. Then whisk in the olive oil, slowly, so it can emulsify well. Taste it, for balance and for salt, then add a couple of drops of cold water and whisk that into the mix, to smooth and further emulsify the dressing. Finish with some pepper. Store in a sealed container in the refrigerator for up to 2 weeks.

VARIATION: You can add a little garlic to the vinaigrette, but do not let the garlic sit in it for more than a day, or it will overwhelm the taste. You can also add some lemon juice or lime juice, but those are best used at the moment of serving. If you want to add an herb, try basil, mint, oregano, or thyme. Add them to the greens and then dress the salad. In the winter, and in the heat of summer, I will often add very thin slices—the tiniest ribbons—of peperoncini to bring bright color and a spike of heat to the vinaigrette.

STOCK

Everyone has told you the virtues and ease of making your own stock, be it chicken, vegetable, beef, or seafood. The taste is subtle and distinct and fresh. But making stock is often the last thing on a to-do list.

The true advantage of your own stock is that you are involved in the details—you choose the pan, the method, the ingredients, the resolution, and the storage. It is not a difficult task, but let no one tell you that it does not involve some mess and a bit of attention.

At home, we have a system for chicken stock making. If we buy a whole chicken, then we always make stock. And if we make stock, then we always have, first, soup with noodles and, a day or so later, risotto. The soup may change each time, and the risotto as well, but we always make them one right after another, as a specific form of a menu. I do not think about it; the parts are simply linked to a result. It is a sequence that promises certain tastes and certain qualities that I cannot otherwise achieve. And that unfolding—the whole chicken, to the stock, to the soup, to the risotto—brings an inevitable efficiency to the process. If there is still stock left, we freeze it for meals that need a boost or for sauces that we have not yet imagined.

One meal signals to the others. It is the context of making the stock that diffuses any sense that it is too complicated. In a more literal analysis, what better use can you imagine for bones and carcass, trimmings and stems, soft carrots and the last limb of celery? The stock is your pot of last resorts and last chances. Use it to clean your fridge, to scrape your cutting boards, to freshen your pantry.

Chicken Stock

1 medium onion, halved

1 carrot, chopped

1 celery stalk, chopped

1 bay leaf

1 cooked chicken carcass, or 4 to 6 pieces bone-in, skin-on cooked chicken pieces

Sea salt and fresh ground black pepper

MAKES 5 TO 6 CUPS (1.2 TO 1.4 L)

The stock will keep for three days in the refrigerator or for a month in the freezer. We like to freeze it in clean large plastic yogurt containers—a few minutes defrosting and the cylinder of frozen soup slides right out. In addition to the ingredients listed here, throw in any trimmings from chopping vegetables.

Put all the ingredients except the salt and pepper in a stockpot and add 3 to 4 quarts (720 to 960 ml) water. Bring it slowly to a boil. Turn the heat down to maintain a low simmer. Froth and impurities will float to the surface; skim them off.

The stock will be ready in 1 hour, but it will be better if left to simmer gently for 2 to 3 hours. You may need to add some fresh water and stir every half hour, but otherwise leave it on its own. When it is ready, let it cool a bit and pour it through a strainer into a large bowl or clean pot, discarding the solids. Let the stock cool, then season it well with salt and pepper. Transfer the cooled stock to storage containers and refrigerate—the stock will keep for three days in the refrigerator. Once chilled, the chicken fat will rise to the surface, and you can easily spoon it off before using the stock.

Vegetable Stock

2 tablespoons extra-
virgin olive oil

1 medium onion,
chopped

2 medium carrots,
chopped

1 pound (455 g) or less
Swiss chard, chopped

2 celery stalks, chopped

Other characters:
fresh or frozen
peas, tomato halves,
leftover parsley or
cilantro, mushrooms,
cauliflower, fennel,
lettuce, broccoli
(optional, if you have
them)

1 or 2 potatoes,
peeled and coarsely
chopped

1 bay leaf

Fresh thyme or
rosemary

Sea salt and fresh
cracked black pepper

MAKES 4 TO 5 CUPS (960 ML TO 1.2 L)

The best homemade stock, at least in relation to its commercial alternative, is vegetable. Commercial vegetable stock is awful. We use whatever vegetable has made it through the week, once fresh or cooked. Do not add beets or Brussel sprouts or asparagus (their tastes are too dominant), but other than that, toss it in. If the parsley looks deflated, or the half-onion puckered—perfect, in it goes.

Heat a stockpot over medium heat. Add the olive oil, onion, carrots, chard, and celery, and as they sweeten and soften, add the other characters and the potato.

Add 10 cups water (2.5 L), the bay leaf, some sprigs of thyme or rosemary, and bring to a boil. Turn down the heat to maintain a very slow simmer, only just bubbling, and cook for 1 hour.

Discard the bay leaf. Taste and adjust the seasoning—the stock will need salt and cracked pepper, sometimes a little more than you might expect. Once it has cooled, strain the liquid, discarding the solids, and decant the stock into glass jars or clean yogurt containers. The stock will keep in the refrigerator for 3 to 4 days, but it freezes well for up to 6 weeks and defrosts quite quickly.

WATER

There are some cultures that cherish their water. In Wellington, New Zealand, there is an artesian well in front of one of its best food shops, with fresh clean bottles next to it. Anyone is welcome to fill up a bottle with the water, at no cost. The bottled water served on Air New Zealand flights comes from one specific spring on the South Island—everyone in the region knows where it is. In France, they will talk about their waters, about their different tastes and properties, as if they were a food. The French will visit certain regions simply to taste the waters, as they would wines.

But in most cultures, water is more a given than a specific, and there might even be an implication that taking water seriously is an indulgence. What is probably most important is that everyone should drink more of it, especially with food and with wines and coffee.

When we serve water with a meal, we serve it in open pitchers or, even better, in long-necked bottles. If people can see the water, and if it is available, they will drink more of it. If we use a great deal of ice, they will drink less. If we flavor the water, with mint or lemon, everyone will try it, but then it seems to not quite fit to the tastes of what is being served. If we store the filled water pitchers in the refrigerator, they will take on some of the tastes that are sitting in the fridge—like the broccoli or the cheese—and then, naturally, people will drink less of the water. Water is best suited to being a trusted and unadorned ally. Sometimes it simply needs a little nudge to get out on the stage.

I use drops of water to set my salad dressings, half ladles of water to make a sauce in a roasting pan, a tablespoon or two to smooth a bubbling pot of beans. It is the first liquid in all cooking, and the first to be taken for granted.

ALCOHOL

White, Red, and Rosé

I do not want to recommend wines. I want to recommend that you try a little wine—that you fiddle with it a bit and find what you enjoy.

There are many wine salesmen out there who will gladly lead you to the popular vintages. One current favorite is what I call knee-buckling reds—red wines that are too strong, 14 percent alcohol and higher. Washington state was enamored of the high-alcohol, tannin-loaded reds for several years, until they discovered, or I hope they discovered, that no one was laughing and many were asleep.

A good red wine has many tasks, among them sociability and grace and even humor. No one talks about such details, but if you mention, say, that you would like a red wine of grace and humor to a wine merchant, you might be surprised. It is a subtlety, but it is not unheard of. And in France, Italy, or Spain, it is almost measurable and certainly understood.

For white wines, we often will ask, with some tongue in cheek, for "rain off the roof" whites; that is, whites that are as clear as running water, cold and direct. Some will act puzzled, but the best shops or stewards seem to know quite directly what it all means.

And for rosés, those wonderful pink wines, you have only to ask that they be dry. Start with the palest rosés before a meal, and move toward the russet rosés as you are ready to eat. They are the spirit of the Mediterranean, from Croatia to Spain, a wine to represent the southern sun, to signal the breezes and the hillsides and the pleasures.

Apéritif

There is a small, precise elegance to *les apéritifs*, the lovely drinks before a meal has even started. I remember when I saw great billboards for Martini & Rossi and Campari in Milan and wondered, Who drinks those? I remember my wife ordering a martini in Frankfurt and getting a Martini & Rossi, with a twist.

They are subtleties, these drinks before. They are more a signal to your system, *let us begin the dinner*, than a signal, *let us party*. Somehow, they set your appetite: Campari, soda, and a twist, or the same for Martini & Rossi. Or Lillet, on the rocks with a twist, all sounding very continental.

But I remember well when you could not even use the word *pasta* and not sound pretentious. *Les apéritifs* are as subtle as using true Parmesan cheese, and with luck, their time is slowly coming around.

Digestifs

But apéritifs' moment may not arrive before the digestifs, which have suddenly become very popular. I have been sipping, after dinner, from a bottle of Averna, the wonderful Italian digestif, for a couple of years. Last month, we hosted a post-wedding party for three young couples and they drank all of it. Averna, we love Averna!

The digestifs are their own mystery. Typically, they are of a higher alcohol content, but even more particularly, they are a distillation from herbs and spices and secrecy. They can even, like a Fernet Branca, make no effort at all to taste palatable or even sociable.

In Italy, the most popular digestifs are the *amari*. There are dozens of labels, Fernet Branca and Averna among them, all from the amaro family of bitter liqueurs. Some are quite light and are better served before dinner. Aperol, for example, is used typically in a spritzer, with a little Prosecco and soda, a slice of orange, and let us wait for dinner.

But many are classic digestifs, like Ramazzotti or Averna or the wonderful Montenegro, that are rarely mixed with anything. They are the drink of reflection, typically poured in a smaller glass, slightly sweet and slightly bitter. They are the drink as you look back on the meal— or as you simply look back. A true digestif implies, *I will help with the meal and you can take a moment.*

THE FIVE DAIRY PRODUCTS

Parmigiano-Reggiano / Feta / Butter /

Yogurt / Five Other Cheeses

PARMIGIANO-REGGIANO

The 1950s, in the United States and in much of the world, were particularly dark years for the food industry. The postwar instincts for modernism extended to everything from bread to green beans—everything would be homogenized, pasteurized, commodified, and available.

Actual Parmigiano cheese all but disappeared in this country, as a fact and as a notion. Instead, Parmesan cheese became an invented product, made in Wisconsin, not a *Parmigiano* cheese at all—pregrated, sold in green paper containers, and kept at room temperature. We would shake it out onto our red sauce.

Today, we are fortunate to have brighter, subtler days in regard to cooking and food. But these are clever times. Now the threat to Parmigiano is not that it might disappear, but that the imitations of it are remarkably deceptive and contrived. They have perfect names—Parmigiano, Parmesan, Parmesano—but the imitations are products of food and chemical invention.

There is one Parmigiano-Reggiano, only one. It is made in the region of Emilia-Romagna, from milk that must be drawn that day, and made with the addition of salt and rennet, a natural enzyme, and nothing else. The wheel of cheese will be aged for twelve months and not sold before eighteen months. The very name *Parmesan*, a literal English translation of Parmigiano, is licensed and protected in Europe. If you ask for Parmesan, you must get Parmigiano-Reggiano; it is the law.

If you are in a restaurant and they ask if you would like more Parmesan cheese, it is nearly certain they are not serving actual Parmigiano cheese. If they are smiling, holding a bowl of grated cheese and big spoon to serve it in abundance, then it is certainly not real Parmesan cheese. It is a pretender, often sweet and a little gummy. It is fine—it will melt and add a cheese taste, but call it not Parmesan.

If you want to set a taste line for Parmesan, and get a sense of its brilliance and understand better why it is called the king of Italian cheese, then buy a very large chunk, still attached to the rind, from a trustworthy shop. The outer skin must say, in repetition, Parmigiano-Reggiano, and there must be a DOP stamp of authenticity and a stamp of month and year of production. There may be a few options, mostly in terms of age, but start with the youngest Parmesan.

A young Parmesan is at least twelve months old, a prime Parmesan is twenty-four months old, and a mature Parmesan is thirty-six months old. The price, of course, dutifully follows the aging process. For most purposes, the younger Parmesan is quite perfect. The prime two-year-old Parmesan is a luxury, and the mature Parmesan is an exception, to be eaten perhaps after a meal, as a celebration, with a perfect pear or strawberry or a slight drizzle of honey.

When you unwrap your cheese, you will smell the Parmesan. Using a short, blunt knife, you should lever off a few small pieces. True Parmesan is slightly crumbly and will break off like soft rock or shale—it is never a gummy mass. Taste the small irregular pieces; they will be a little salty, fine-grained, and delicious. They never taste better than when first cut, and the table scraps left over from cutting a hunk of Parmesan into smaller portions are a taste you will remember.

Once you have true Parmesan, then you can use it with a sure, and even haughty, confidence. Grated into a soup or pasta, coating broccoli or asparagus, sprinkled across roasted vegetables, stirred into a sauce, it is a taste protected, refined, and detailed by a thousand-year-old process.

Parmigiano-Reggiano and the Egg

1 tablespoon white
vinegar

1 large fresh organic
egg

2 slices thick country
bread

2 tablespoons unsalted
butter

¼ pound (115 g) chunk
of fresh Parmigiano-
Reggiano

Salt and fresh cracked
black pepper

SERVES 1

**Sometimes, if I have good fresh eggs, some country bread, and a
fresh piece of Parmesan, I will make this, late at night or early in
the morning, and remind myself again of the precise pleasure
of true Parmesan.**

Bring a shallow saucepan of water to a boil. Add the vinegar, turn
the heat off, and gently crack the egg into the pan. Cover and let it
rest for 4 minutes, precisely.

Meanwhile, toast the bread, butter it well, and lay a slice on a
warmed plate. Take the poached egg out with a slotted spoon,
and lay it on one slice of bread. Quickly, while the egg is hot, grate
some of the cheese over the whole piece so it can slightly melt.
Grate the cheese generously. You will not need the whole piece of
cheese—the extra is in case other people see you and want one.

Salt and pepper it well, cut into four sections, and enjoy. The extra
bread is for mop-up.

FETA

In some ways, feta and Parmesan have much in common. They are each a distinct product and even a symbol of their countries. They are each a cultural response to particular needs and resources, and they are intimately connected to their cuisines and to their lands.

Crumbled white feta signals Greek sheep and goats, rocky hillsides and whitewashed buildings, herbs and salty ocean air. Parmesan signals green, grassy fields and herds of cattle, stacks of air-drying yellow wheels of cheese, wheat, and flour.

At its best, and freshest, feta has the unusual combination of being both slightly wet and slightly crumbly. You should always be able to taste the salt and, right behind it, the sheep's milk. Typically, it will be described as firm or as soft. The firm is the higher grade, and the soft is spreadable, like ricotta.

It is not an expensive cheese—it is not meant to be. The production is not impossibly complicated. It is a people's cheese, meant for daily use, for a sprinkle or a taste or an influence, but principally for its representation, both visually and in taste, of freshness. In a sense, feta is a signal of victory over hard land and rock and ocean. The lovely white crumbles of feta are the dance and ingenuity of Greek cuisine.

Use feta with everything from strawberries to lamb, pizza to green beans to peaches. There are few places that it would not be comfortable and gracious. It loves the company of tortillas or pitas. You can use it quite plainly or with olive oil, herbs, and fresh chopped greens.

Feta and a Simple Snack

1 small red onion, sliced

Sea salt and fresh
ground black pepper

2 tablespoons extra-
virgin olive oil, plus
more as needed

1 cup (190 g) cooked
rice (or lentils,
couscous, quinoa, or
beans, or a mixture
of any of these)

6 pitas or small corn
tortillas or good
sliced bread, crusts
removed

4 ounces (115 g) fresh
feta, crumbled

2 tablespoons plain
Greek yogurt

1 tablespoon hummus

6 to 8 slices avocado,
with some lemon
juice squeezed on
them

1 tomato, coarsely
chopped and salted

¼ cup (10 g) chopped
fresh cilantro

¼ cup (40 g) Kalamata
or Taggiasca olives,
pitted and coarsely
chopped

1 lemon, halved

1 sprig fresh oregano or
thyme, or a couple
fresh basil leaves

SERVES 4

We might serve this before dinner or late in the afternoon. It does not, of course, need rice specifically. It could also work with cooked lentils or beans, couscous or quinoa—whatever is handy. It is the feta that makes everyone look good. Be careful to have a plan or reason that you cannot keep making more of the snack, or you will be making it for an hour. This dish lures an appetite more than fills it up.

Heat a cast-iron pan over medium-low heat for 20 minutes or so.

At the same time, soak the onion in salted water for 20 minutes, then drain and dry on paper towels. Chop it a little and put it in a small bowl with some salt and pepper and a little of the olive oil.

Heat a medium saucepan over low heat. Add a little of the olive oil and sauté the rice for a minute or two, to loosen it and take the chill off. You might add a tablespoon or so of water to the pan as it reheats.

Add a little olive oil to the preheated cast-iron pan, swirl it about to coat the surface, and put the pitas in the pan to heat. Turn them after a minute or two. They might brown a little, but you are trying to heat rather than sear them. If the pan is too hot, turn down the heat—too much heat will stiffen the pita.

Working quickly, lay one pita on each warmed plate. Add a little olive oil, a small sprinkle of feta, some salt, and then dabs of yogurt, hummus, and the rice. Lay an avocado slice across and top with some of the onion, tomato, cilantro, olives, and a squeeze of lemon.

Finish with the oregano, some salt and pepper, a drizzle of olive oil, and more feta and serve immediately.

BUTTER

No one really talks about butter anymore, but they still use it, and it can always use a little attention. It is fashionable to not be very fashionable about butter—to keep a couple of anonymous sticks in the fridge, sticks that have the secondhand appeal of old gym shorts.

I am picky about butter. I would rather use less of a more expensive butter than not use very much because it is not very good. For daily use, I choose a cultured butter like Plugrá, either salted or not. I never put it all out on the table, especially if there is a good loaf of bread being served. Instead, I will slice off a piece, lay that on small plate, and then detail it a little with flaky salt. The salt has a wonderful ability to slow matters down. People will use less butter and taste it more specifically.

Or I make a compound butter. I lop off a chunk of butter, let that soften, and then mix into it some favorites: lemon juice and lemon zest, or rosemary and thyme, or parsley and basil, always a little extra salt. Then I pack the compound butter into small ramekins and know they will not be gulped in one pass at the table. Or I freeze the mixed butter and use it to finish a grilled piece of fish or meat.

Butter is a brilliant finisher to dishes, especially pasta, rice, and sauces. But when using it to finish a dish, make certain the butter is very cold, even frozen, or it will have a tendency to separate. Once your risotto is just right, stir in small chunks of very cold butter, to smooth and sweeten the rice. And as you are deglazing a pan that cooked a chicken or a roast, using stock or simply water, add butter at the very end to bring the elements of the sauce together.

Pasta with Sage and Butter, Alone

Sea salt

½ pound (225 g)
   fresh ravioli or good-
   quality dried pasta
   like pappardelle,
   cavatelli, or penne
   rigate

4 tablespoons
   (½ stick/55 g) cold,
   unsalted butter

6 to 8 fresh sage leaves

½ cup (50 g) freshly
   grated Parmigiano-
   Reggiano cheese

Fresh ground black
   pepper

SERVES 4, AS A LIGHT STARTER

If I have good butter and six fresh sage leaves and some Parmesan cheese, I will often make a pasta from the three of them, plus salt, of course. And I always marvel at how good this simple dish is.

Whichever pasta you choose, pay attention to its recommended cooking time. The fresh ravioli will be ready much quicker than the dried varieties. Make certain the pasta finishes cooking just as the sauce is ready.

Bring a large pot of water to a boil. Add a good pinch of salt and the ravioli. Cook the pasta according to the package instructions, draining it a minute or so before the recommended cooking time. You must undercook it slightly; it will cook further in the sauce.

While the ravioli cooks, melt the butter in a medium saucepan over medium-low heat. Be careful to only slightly color it—it is not meant to brown. It should take only a couple of minutes.

Add the sage leaves, turn them over once or twice to coat them in the butter. Add some salt, stir, and take the pan off the heat for a moment. The sauce is done.

Drain the pasta quickly, reserving ¼ cup (60 ml) of the pasta cooking water. Add the pasta to the pan with the sage butter and set the pan over low heat. Stir gently and slowly add the reserved pasta water. It should thicken a little in the heat, but you must only be on the heat for 2 minutes at the most or the pasta will be overcooked. Taste and adjust the seasoning.

Add the cheese and some pepper and stir again. You have a simple tour de force—cow's-milk butter, leading a merry band of one herb, one cow's-milk cheese, and a little bit of pasta. Serve in warmed pasta bowls (be sure they are warm, or the sauce will deflate).

YOGURT

These are days of renaissance for yogurt, and rightly so. It has emerged from countless health campaigns and now finally seems to be on a path of full acceptance into food cultures.

It is the full acceptance that is new. Yogurt itself has been a staple for much of the world for a thousand years. Iceland, Nepal, Iran, India, Turkey, Greece—all have long records of yogurt in their cuisines, the thickened milk made slightly sour with the addition of bacteria, the bacteria causing fermentation and extending the life of the milk.

Yogurt's rise in popularity in the United States was helped in part by the emergence of Greek yogurt, a style that seems to celebrate a better nature. Greek yogurt is simply yogurt that has been strained—in the most basic version, it is yogurt that has sat in muslin until much of the whey has drained away. It is thicker, almost cleaner or symbolically purer, and it seems best suited to less sugar and more natural fruit or honey as additions to it. Greek yogurt does not separate. It remains compact and has but a slight trail of milky liquid. It can be spooned onto a plate or toasted bread with less concern that it will release a trail of moisture.

I use many kinds of yogurt, Greek and others, depending on the task. If I am mixing yogurt into a sauce or soup or dressing, then I will use a natural yogurt, unsweetened, and my concern will be focused on where the milk came from and what were the cows eating. If the yogurt is to be mixed with grains or herbs or oils or condiments and such, I will typically use a Greek yogurt, knowing it will better hold its shape.

A Yogurt Sauce

1 good sprig fresh dill

6 fresh mint leaves

Sea salt and fresh
ground black pepper

2 garlic cloves, minced

1 tablespoon extra-
virgin olive oil

1 cup (240 ml) plain
unsweetened Greek
yogurt

MAKES 1 CUP (240 ML)

This is a very simple sauce. Use the sauce as an appetizer, with toasted breads and crackers, or alongside grilled fish and chicken. I am always amazed what a pleasure it is. Hats off to yogurt, waiting with such patience.

Chop the dill and mint together with some salt and pepper. Stir the garlic and olive oil into the yogurt, then stir in the herbs. Season with salt and pepper. If not using immediately, store in an airtight container and it will keep in the refrigerator for 3 days at least.

VARIATIONS: I have also made this by stirring the garlic and herbs in first and pouring the olive oil over the yogurt and then seasoning it. It creates a different image—that of the yellow-green olive oil sitting atop the very white yogurt.

If serving the sauce with a hearty base like lentils or rice, or with beans, you can lead it in a very different direction by exchanging the dill and mint for mustard seeds and cumin seeds. Heat 2 teaspoons each of mustard seeds and cumin seeds together in a small frying pan over medium heat for 5 minutes or so. Crush them a little with a wooden spoon, then add them to the yogurt with the garlic and olive oil. It will give a fine edge to the sauce.

FIVE OTHER CHEESES

We do not eat much cheese at the shop, unless it should arrive at a perfect moment, and then we seem to eat it all. But that is the nature of cheese. If it is served too cold, or with the wrong wine, or at the wrong time, or even inelegantly, the cheese can sit stubbornly and unhumorously alone. There are few more glamorous moments for cheeses than when they are on display in the glass case of a cheese shop. They all look quite wonderful, sharing the spotlight and the attention. Their bodies shine; their skin and rind seem subtle records of time and preparation and care.

When you get one, or several, of them home, you must do a bit of retailing, and you must give each of them some consideration. You cannot simply unwrap each delicacy and square and plop them on a large plate. I have seen brilliant subtle cheeses go untouched because they sat next to a gooey triple crème that took all the attention. There is a proper knife for hard cheeses, but that knife will make a mess of soft cheeses. The softer cheeses need time and warmth to even get soft. The pairing, the cutlery, the serving dish, the temperature, and the size of the slice all deserve some thought.

We ordered cheese from a wonderful farm here in Puget Sound, Kurtwood Farms, to help celebrate a book launch. They brought three small platters, each with the same three cheeses on them, in small portions. And, beneath the cheeses, they lined the platters with the waxy leaves of the bay tree. When the event was over, there were only bay leaves left. The smaller portions had helped each platter serve and show itself.

When you are at a cheese shop and ask for a taste, you get a very small sliver and you concentrate to perceive the taste. In a sense, that is what you want to reenact when you serve cheese—that the person will concentrate and that the unique flavors will be perceptible. Perhaps the best way to serve cheese is to literally serve it to each person. If it is a selection, then cut a small piece of each and carefully set it on the plate. If a single cheese, then add two or three cuts.

I would not add anything pickled to the plate, but I might add a small teaspoon of a chutney or a sweet quince jam—or a couple of slices of apple or pear. Sometimes, I will put a small plate of fresh crackers out, or very thinly sliced toasted bread, but never a fresh, thick slice of bread—that takes up too much room in the confines of taste and hunger.

A cheddar must crumble, a tomme will slice, a chèvre will share, a Brie will soften. That is how they stand best—some are shy, some love a party, some love guests, and some love to simply sing all by themselves. Getting to know their characteristics is part of the process.

Here are five cheeses that we use often. Three are local to Puget Sound and Washington and two are from far away. They work wonderfully, both before and after meals, but they are not the only choices, and sometimes not even the best choices. To me, it makes sense to start with your local cheeses. They reflect where you are, your land, your water. It is easy enough to be lured by the faraway and hard to appreciate how good things can be just up the road.

- *Dinah's Cheese*
- *Casatica di Bufala*
- *Island Brebis*
- *Fromage d'Affinois*
- *Fresh Goat's-Milk Chèvre*

THE FIVE BREADS

Pita / Baguette / Ciabatta /
Rustic Loaf / Tortillas

PITA

I looked in the supermarket and there were eight different makers of pita or Syrian bread or Arabic flatbread, three of the most common names for this wonderful flatbread. Some seemed more whole wheat than others, but they were all quite similar.

Pita is the people's bread and a wonderful staple in the Mediterranean and Middle East with at least a four-thousand-year-long history. I use pita every week—either as hors d'oeuvres with a sauce or two or as an important ally to a light supper. I can lay out yogurt and a little hummus, some sliced vegetables and marinated onions or carrots, a little chopped greens, some lime and cilantro, some chopped tomatoes, a half cup of cooked rice, and perhaps some extra lentils, and know that the pita will help make all the parts seem welcome (see also pages 45 and 168).

Pita is a combination of white and whole-wheat flours, water, salt, and olive oil. The flours are mixed into a light yeast base, kneaded for a couple of minutes, and left to rise. Later they are separated into smaller pieces, to rise again and then be flattened to individual sizes.

These are cooked on any oven surface, cast iron or stone, for just a few minutes. The quick kneading, the very soft and moist dough, and the multiple risings make the pita very supple, and the heat causes each piece to puff up as it is baked. It is the puffing up that creates the pocket between the layers.

Like any bread, there is a great difference between the industrial version and the artisanal version of pita. We have a wonderful Syrian restaurant, Mamnoon, nearby, and they have very conscientiously perfected a system for making their own pita bread. We have never gone to Mamnoon and not collected a bag of their pitas.

Pita Bread

2 teaspoons active dry yeast

Pinch of sugar

1 tablespoon whole-wheat flour

2 cups plus 2 tablespoons (265 g) unbleached all-purpose flour, plus more for dusting

1 teaspoon sea salt

2 tablespoons extra-virgin olive oil, plus more for greasing

MAKES 8 PIECES

Commercial pita is easily available. But it can also be made at home, even without a proper oven. In certain ways, it is best if made spontaneously and less officiously than with industrial ovens and preparation. It is part of the very history of pita that it be possible and doable and a pleasure to make the pita at home— to smell the fresh dough cooking in your own oven. And if you let the pita cool for 5 minutes after baking, you will have time to lightly toast some sesame seeds. Add them plus a pinch of dried thyme and oregano and salt to 2 tablespoons of olive oil. Mix and then dip the fresh pita into the herbs and oil. You have done it!

In a small, warmed bowl, stir together the yeast, sugar, and 1 cup (240 ml) warm water. Add the whole-wheat flour and 2 table-spoons of the all-purpose flour. Stir well with a fork and let the mixture sit someplace warm for 10 minutes or so, until the yeast begins to bubble.

In a large bowl, combine the remaining 2 cups (250 g) all-purpose flour and the salt. Make a well in the center and, with a good rub-ber spatula, scrape the bubbling yeast mixture into the well. Pour the olive oil on top.

Working around the bowl, scrape and blend the flour to combine it with the yeast mixture until it forms a loose clump. Add a pinch more flour to your hands and reach in and knead the dough four or five times, just to bring it all together.

Lay the dough on a floured surface and knead it well for 5 minutes or so, until it smooths a bit. You are making pita bread, not French bread, so do not overwork the dough or add much flour—it must remain elastic and a little tacky.

Clean the bowl in which you mixed the dough. Grease it very lightly with olive oil and put the dough in it. Cover with plastic wrap and a dishtowel and set it in a warm place (e.g., high in a cupboard) to rise. In an hour or so, the dough should have doubled in size.

Preheat the oven to 500°F (260°C). Put a pizza stone or a good stiff baking sheet on the bottom rack to heat.

Punch down the dough. Turn it out of the bowl onto a floured surface. With a scraper or spatula, divide the dough into eight pieces. Round them a little and let the pieces rest on the floured surface for 10 minutes, with a dishtowel draped over them to prevent drying.

Flatten one of the pieces and roll it out to an 8-inch (20-cm) circle. With a spatula, transfer the dough to the oven, on the hot surface, and bake for 2 minutes on one side and 1 minute on the other. It should puff a bit, brown a little, smell quite wonderful, and be baked through. Repeat with the remaining dough.

The cooked bread can be stored in a zip-top bag for 1 or 2 days. It is easily reheated in a warm oven or a warmed frying pan. Should you have any dough left, store it in a small bowl, with a little olive oil coating the dough and plastic wrap sealing the top, and refrigerate. You can store the dough for 1 day before cooking.

BAGUETTE

When I first arrived in Seattle in 1970, there were a couple of industrial bakeries, but no one was making bread by hand. Handmade bread was like making your own pie crust, like making your own soup, like making pancakes from scratch. Bread by hand was simply old-fashioned, and this country was going to clean up old-fashioned and get on with the new.

It may well have been the very first Starbucks, in the Pike Place Market, that signaled change was en route. Before Starbucks, coffee was not made to your order in the United States. In fact, it was made whether you ordered it or not. But suddenly, each cup was specific, and, for the most part, handmade. And, for the most part, better. The very mechanics of a cappuccino were, in a sense, revolutionary and personal and artisanal.

It soon followed in Seattle that people would also want bread that was personal. The breads were more expensive than the industrial brand and certainly more variable, but they also had more taste. By the 1990s, Seattle had three kinds of baguette—a very white, and light, French baguette; a more yellow semolina baguette; and a denser rustic baguette, with a little whole-wheat and rye flour added to it.

We often ask of a town, "Where are the good restaurants?" But it is just as indicative to ask, "Where are the best bakeries and what are they best at?" I have lived in towns that had no bread. And I have seen how even one good bakery can improve the spirit and even confidence of a neighborhood. Good bread is important.

Croutons on Their Own Fine Merit

1 or 2 baguettes, fresh or day-old

½ cup (120 ml) extra-virgin olive oil, plus more as needed

Sea salt and fresh ground black pepper

Optional additions: red pepper flakes, fresh thyme, fresh oregano, finely chopped pancetta, chopped garlic, minced carrot, minced celery, minced fennel, chopped chives, freshly grated Parmigiano-Reggiano

¼ cup (13 g) chopped fresh flat-leaf parsley

MAKES 2 CUPS (60 G)

For a time, we had an arrangement with a local bakery. They would exchange what bread was left by the afternoon for children's books. Their staff had young families and we had plenty of young eaters. Several times, we would simply have too many baguettes—that is when I learned to serve fresh croutons, all by themselves. You could put the pieces into a salad, but they work just as well as an appetizer and snack. You can send the bread off into other places with a wide variety of extra ingredients, from garlic to vegetables to cheese. Croutons love company.

Preheat the oven to 275°F (135°C).

Trim the crust from the baguette(s). Cut the trimmed loaf (or loaves) into roughly 1-inch (2.5-cm) squares.

Spread the cut bread pieces out on a rimmed baking sheet and toast in the oven for 10 minutes to dry them. Turn them a little and toast for 5 minutes more, then remove and let cool.

Put the bread in a big stainless-steel bowl and pour in half the olive oil, shaking or stirring to mix and coat the bread with the oil. Toss again with a good sprinkle of salt and pepper.

Heat a large sauté pan over medium-low heat. Add the remaining olive oil, and when that gets hot, add any optional ingredients you're using, except for Parmesan or fresh herbs.

Add the bread. Let it sit for a minute or two and then give it a shake. If the pieces have not started to brown, the temperature might be too low. They should brown in 6 to 8 minutes, but you should toss them every minute or so. When they are nearly done, add some of the chopped parsley and a little more pepper.

When the bread cubes are all browned, turn them out onto a wide dinner plate or serving plate so they have a little room. Add some salt, the rest of the parsley, and a handful of grated Parmesan cheese or fresh herbs (if using). Toss it all together. You might even need one last flourish of a little olive oil over the top of everything.

The croutons can be stored in an airtight container for at least a couple of days.

CIABATTA

I used to assume that the Italian bakers invented and perfected the ciabatta many years ago. It is so like them—a sporty, floury roll. The word *ciabatta* means "slipper"—the loaves and rolls are shaped like a man's slipper, slightly domed and slightly flat and wider than a typical loaf.

A ciabatta has not the smooth, tubular shape of a French baguette. It has a more workmanlike surface. It is always dusted with flour and appears as if it has not quite fully risen to what it might have become. In shape, it is more like a mound of pizza dough than a sculpted boule.

But in fact the ciabatta, despite its rustic appearances, was designed and invented in the 1980s, as a defense against and answer to the French baguette, which was dominating the then-new craze and lust for panini sandwiches.

It can be grilled and pressed and toasted and fried, and it will still retain a pliable interior and the slightly crispy crust. The ciabatta can seem almost sweet, but it is not typically made with any sugar, except perhaps in the starter. It is literally sweet with flour. A perfect ciabatta loaf is made with very hard wheat, which produces very high-gluten flour. Neapolitan pizza dough is similarly produced with flour from hard wheat.

The ciabatta is built, in a sense, to work. It has a spongy, holey interior, soft and varied. And it has a slightly crispy crust. As a result, it is quite brilliant for a panini, or for an open sandwich or bruschetta. The cheeses, tomatoes, olive oil, and chopped parsley can slip and tuck within the folds, but the crust will hold the line from leaks.

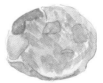

Leftover Ciabatta Snacks

1 medium, ripe tomato, peeled, seeded, and chopped

1 small ripe avocado, peeled, pit removed

Salt and fresh ground black pepper

Tabasco sauce

1 lime

2 tablespoons chopped fresh cilantro

Extra-virgin olive oil, as needed

2 ciabatta rolls or 1 loaf

1 garlic clove, peeled

SERVE 3 TO 4 AS AN APPETIZER

We buy ciabatta rolls in the morning and make fresh sandwiches with them for lunch. By dinnertime, any extra rolls are a little hard. But they are still wonderful—you simply need to get creative.

Heat a cast-iron pan on medium.

Put the chopped tomato and the avocado in separate small bowls—add salt and pepper and a dash of Tabasco to each, a squeeze of lime, some of the cilantro, and a few drops of olive oil as well. With a fork, mix the bowls separately, mashing the avocado as you do.

Cut the ciabatta rolls in half lengthwise (if it is a ciabatta loaf, cut 2-inch/5-cm slices). Add 1 tablespoon of the olive oil to the pan, wait a moment for it to heat, and then put the ciabatta, cut side down, into the pan, as many as will fit.

You are simply browning the ciabatta, not frying the pieces, so keep the heat up and do not use too much of the oil. Turn each piece as it browns. When both sides are done, put the pieces onto a cutting board and quickly rub one side with the garlic and add a slight drizzle of olive oil.

Now dress the pieces with either the tomato or the avocado mix or even a combination. Use all that you have—then add salt and pepper and whatever cilantro is left, another dash of Tabasco, a squeeze of lime, and a final line of olive oil.

With a sharp knife, cut each ciabatta into four pieces of any shape, and lay them all on a wide plate. Scrape anything left on the cutting board over the pieces, and serve.

RUSTIC LOAF

There is a fine new fashion rolling through bread baking—the rustic loaf, a big, 2- to 3-pound (910-g to 1.4-kg) mound of bread. It is expensive ($6 to $8 per loaf) and stubborn. It is, in its way, a Viking throwback, for it makes no apologies. It needs its own bag, it makes a mess when you cut it, and it dominates the counter. There have been big loaves before, but they were simply big-sized. These rustic loaves are big-boned as well, thick and thick-crusted.

For all its oomph and crustiness, the rustic loaf is a fine piece of bread, especially the first couple of days. It is not spongy, but sort of begrudgingly soft inside. The mess aside, the slices are wonderful, and their taste so obvious that you can plow right through two or three slices without the lure of salty butter.

You can serve the bread for at least two days as a fresh loaf. Wrap the extra bread in aluminum foil. If you serve the slices, supply some good butter, even some with a little salt added to it. That is one of the highlights of this loaf. The rustic loaf also freezes well, the denseness of the bread protecting it.

By the end of the second day, you can begin making plans for the next presentation. It makes superb toast—again with some butter, but also with cream cheese. And for lunch and dinner, the toasted bread, rubbed with a halved garlic clove and coated with olive oil and salt and pepper, is perfect as an ally to a soup. The toast is the perfect surface for some mashed avocado (see page 71), served to the side of a meal.

Your $6 to $8 investment starts to look good by those second and third days. To me, it looks especially good when I am having a piece of toast, and, crumbs aside, I am pleased with the solid company.

Grilled Cheese Sandwich with Avocado

2 tablespoons extra-
    virgin olive oil, plus
    more as needed

2 large slices of bread
    from a rustic loaf

8 slices ripe avocado

4 ounces (115 g)
    mozzarella cheese

Pinch of dried oregano

Sea salt and fresh
    ground black pepper

4 slices ripe tomato
    (optional)

MAKES 1 SANDWICH

On the third day, assuming you still have some of your rustic loaf, make this sandwich.

Heat a cast-iron pan over medium-high heat. Add half of the olive oil, and when it is hot, add the bread. Grill the slices briefly on the first side, then pull them out of the pan and add a little more olive oil to the grilled sides.

Lay avocado on the grilled side of one piece of bread and the mozzarella on the other piece, and sprinkle some oregano over the cheese. Add some salt and pepper.

Put the two slices together and return them to the pan. Push down hard and grill the first side for 2 to 3 minutes, then flip the sandwich and grill the other side, 2 minutes more. You should see the mozzarella beginning to melt. Lift the sandwich out onto a cutting board and cut it into four triangles.

Serve each triangle with a little olive oil drizzled over it and a slice of fresh tomato, if tomatoes are in season.

TORTILLAS

In America, if you say "tortilla," then you generally mean a wheat-flour tortilla. The gluten of wheat allows the tortilla to bend and fold and gives it a consistency that will keep and shelve and ship quite well. The flour is less expensive than corn maize and considerably less specific as to its origin and process. The flour tortilla is perfect for the burrito or the wrap and, in fact, the tortilla has become more popular in the States than the bagel.

In Mexico, if you say "tortilla," you mean the maize tortilla, made from specially treated corn kernels. The corn is dried and then rehydrated in a calcium solution, which softens the kernels and removes an outer skin. The rehydrated corn is then ground and formed into a pliable dough called *masa*. For all but the northern regions of Mexico, a tortilla is always made from masa and water.

A corn tortilla is smaller and not particularly pliable, nor does it have much more of a shelf life than an afternoon. It is, in a sense, the present tense of much of Mexican cooking. The tortilla is made when it is needed. It is masa, salt, water, and a griddle and, of course, a craft.

A tortilla is a quick bread; there is no yeast or leavening. It is a product of hand labor and subtlety more than of ingredients. That said, the corn tortilla has many variations—of taste, color, and texture—that reflect the type of corn that has been used in its production. The flour tortilla makes no reference to what type of flour has been used, though you can often find "home style" versus conventional, the "home style" having been browned on each side.

Corn or flour tortillas—they are both readily available now, in markets or supermarkets, plastic wrapped 12 to 16 per batch. They will keep best for 2 to 3 days. I try to buy mine from Spanish or Mexican markets, for they are often made locally for that shop.

Fresh Fish Tacos

1 pound (455 g) halibut, snapper, or black cod fillet, skinned, washed, and patted dry (if the fish is more than 2 to 3 inches/5 to 7.5 cm thick, cut in half horizontally)

Sea salt and fresh ground black pepper

2 teaspoons ground hot chile or cayenne

1 teaspoon dried thyme or oregano

1 garlic clove, very finely chopped

2 tablespoons extra-virgin olive oil

12 cherry tomatoes, halved

1 shallot, chopped

1 small serrano chile, chopped

¼ cup (10 g) chopped fresh cilantro, plus sprigs for serving

1 teaspoon white wine vinegar

4 lime wedges

1 ripe avocado

½ cup (10 g) arugula, lightly chopped

6–8 tortillas, corn or flour

SERVES 4

You could make this with any tortilla, but you must be certain the tortilla has been warmed.

Put the fish fillet in a stainless-steel bowl and season well with salt and pepper. Add the chile powder, thyme, and garlic and then most of the olive oil. Rub the mixture into the fish, making sure to coat both sides. Cover the bowl and refrigerate for 2 hours.

In a small bowl, combine the tomatoes, shallot, serrano, a little of the cilantro, the vinegar, the juice of 1 lime wedge, and a seasoning of salt and pepper. Scoop the avocado flesh into a separate shallow bowl. Slice it and sprinkle it with the juice of 1 lime wedge and season with salt and pepper. In a third bowl, salt the arugula lightly and toss it.

Heat a large cast-iron pan over medium-low heat (you could also use a griddle or a stone in the oven—any surface that can warm the tortillas). Heat the tortillas for half a minute on each side to refresh them, then wrap them in a warm towel to keep them soft.

Take the fish out to get the chill off it and lay the pieces out on a platter for 5 minutes or so. Heat a little olive oil in a sauté pan over medium-high. Cook the fish, in batches if need be, for 3 minutes on one side and 2 minutes on the next, just until it firms up. When done, lay the fish on a different platter, one that has been warmed. Sprinkle with the cilantro sprigs and the juice of 1 lime wedge, and season with black pepper.

To assemble the tacos, first place a small piece of fish in the center of a tortilla, then add a little of the tomato and shallot mix, some avocado, a small clump of arugula, the cilantro, and some of the juice of the remaining lime wedge. Repeat with the remaining ingredients and serve immediately.

THE FIVE FRUITS

Tomatoes / Apples / Avocado /

Lemons and Limes

TOMATOES

There are no better canned tomatoes in the world than Italian San Marzano tomatoes. Perhaps they will always be the very best. But I am surprised that there are no other canned tomatoes that are even close.

I can buy wonderful, fresh heirloom tomatoes, starting in the spring. They are best eaten sliced and raw, with a little salt, vinegar, and olive oil. But they do not produce a great tomato sauce. They are too watery and give a slightly bitter taste to the sauce.

And I can buy quite remarkable cherry tomatoes—each one seems able to explode for a moment with the taste and smell of tomato. They do not work in a long sauté, but they work brilliantly if cooked for only a minute or two sometimes with a little spritz of water for steam. Cherry tomatoes are like a firecracker. They are of little use in making a tomato sauce.

There are plum (or Roma) tomatoes in every supermarket and every farmers' market, and plum tomatoes are perfect for making tomato sauce. But somehow, no one has figured out how to grow plum tomatoes that have taste. They are grown for looks only. Their skin is smooth, but quite thick, and their meat is not robust. And they have little taste. But they do keep and they certainly stack atop one another; they are practically Mayan for structure.

It will be a fine subtlety and clear progress when the perceived value of a tomato, particularly a tomato for making a tomato sauce, reaches a level that entices the suppliers to grow such a tomato. We have the wine in this country, we have the olives and the basil and the pasta and the cheese, but the sturdiest element, the tomato, we are still hesitant about. We are hesitant to believe that it is not enough to be simply bright red—you must have taste, as well.

Tomatoes and Sports Bar Green Beans

Sea salt

1 baseball-size Yukon
   Gold potato (any
   thin-skinned variety
   is fine)

1½ pounds (220 g)
   green beans, or
   yellow purple beans,
   or haricots verts,
   trimmed

2 tablespoons plus
   1 teaspoon extra-
   virgin olive oil

1 tablespoon cold,
   unsalted butter

1 pound (350 g) fresh
   cherry tomatoes

1 dried hot chile

1 garlic clove, peeled
   and crushed

Flaky sea salt

Whole black
   peppercorns, roughly
   cracked

12 to 16 basil or Thai
   basil leaves, chopped
   slightly and carefully
   (if you can find no
   basil, you could use
   1 tablespoon of
   pesto, thinned with
   a little hot water)

SERVES 2 TO 4

By midsummer, green beans, cherry tomatoes, and basil are plentiful. This is a fine way to get them all involved. These green beans would easily bump the French fries and quesadillas at your local twelve-screen sports bar, but it will never be a fair fight. I make them as a side dish, a jumble as you would fries, to go with a piece of fish or meat. But more often, I serve them when we are watching some sporting contest. If you make them well and nimbly, they will sit brilliantly at your own table and disappear, just as fries might.

You will slightly taste the garlic and the hot pepper, while the basil will stand out, proud as can be. It is a wonderful chorus for the green beans—even the big muscular ones of summer's end. But do make this dish as well with the thin and elegant haricots verts. They are a little easier to toss about and jumble.

Fill a large saucepan with cold water, add 1 tablespoon of salt and the potato and bring it to a rolling boil. The potato should cook for about 15 minutes, until it is still firm but beginning to soften.

Soak the beans in cold water for 5 minutes, then drain them in a colander. When the potato is slightly softened, pull it out to drain and dry and put the beans right in the boiling water. You are blanching the beans, not cooking them through, so they will need only 2 to 3 minutes of cooking at a full boil. Pull them out and let them rest back in the colander.

When it has cooled a little, cut the potato in half, lay each cut side down and peel back the skin. Then slice the halves no more than ¼ inch (6 mm) thick. You are about to get busy, so choose a nice round large plate or serving dish and put it somewhere that it will get warm—on top of the saucepan with the blanching water would work.

Heat a 12-inch (30.5-cm) sauté pan over medium-high heat for 10 seconds and then add 1 tablespoon of the olive oil and the butter and all of the sliced potato and shake the pan to coat the slices. They should cover the bottom of the pan. Add a good pinch of salt and let the potatoes brown on one side. You can shake the pan to keep them from sticking, but do not turn the potatoes until the one side is browned.

Turn the potatoes and shake the pan again. The stovetop should not be so hot that it is trying to scorch them, but it needs to be hot enough to not slump when the beans hit the pan. Give the potatoes a minute or so (they will be nearly done), and throw in the green beans and some salt and the pepper and toss it all together on the heat. Use tongs and spatula and spoons or your wrist, whatever it takes to get the beans in contact with the heat and the oil and butter. There should be some commotion and noise from the pan.

It all moves quickly at this point. Add 1 tablespoon of olive oil and the cherry tomatoes (see Note). Crumble a little of the hot pepper behind them, and then add the garlic to the olive oil and shake, shake, shake the pan so it is all a jumble in the heat. The whole process from the moment you added the green beans should take no more than 3 minutes—it must be hot and *rapido* or the greens will simply sag in the oil.

With the back of a wooden spoon, squish a couple of the tomatoes to help make a sauce, shake and stir, and suddenly you are done. The green beans should be very hot to the touch but still slightly firm and definitely not limp. The cherry tomatoes should be whole but have slight tears on their skin from the heat, and the potatoes should be crispy. Turn the contents of the pan out onto the warmed platter. Add the last bit of olive oil, some flaky salt, cracked black pepper, and finally the basil leaves.

NOTE: Green beans have many varieties, some more moist than others. If, when you add the cherry tomatoes the pan seems dry, add ¼ cup (60 ml) of hot water as well to create some steam and to help make a small sauce from the deglazing.

APPLES

Apples have become a little like cars. At their newest, and until sold, they shine. You must taste them to find the part that cannot be polished, the fruit itself. Once you find a good one, then I suggest you start plotting how to set a few minutes aside after a meal. Bring in just a piece of a cheese that you like, and start slicing off some of the fruit.

Look at and taste the skin—some are leathery, some are distressed, and some are lovely to eat, but you must do the deciding before you serve. The sticker, with the name and location of the fruit, must never appear at the table—even the scar, where the sticker was removed, must disappear.

There is a lot going on, to serve a simple fruit with cheese, with many small decisions made, quietly and unnoticed, before you serve the plates. You have presented a piece of fruit that has in all likelihood been on a long journey already. You did not bake or smear or glaze it—you brought it out, all by itself, unadorned, the implication: *here, a good piece of fruit.*

If you do it well, give yourself credit. It is a great honor, and a true antidote to a world increasingly trying to ignore its seasons and its very own nature. You have slowed the many false clocks and taken a moment for your own. Bravo.

I do have a routine with apples that I have maintained: I make applesauce. You only need a few tools—a medium or large saucepan, cutting board, sharp knife, and an Italian food mill. The food mill is brilliant with apples. It cares not if you leave the core and seeds and skins on; it cares not if the apples are handsome and peeled or ugly and pockmarked and wormy. It separates all that, and you are left with the soft applesauce.

Applesauce

MAKES 3 CUPS (720 ML)

2 tablespoons unsalted butter

12 to 16 apples, quartered

Pinch of sea salt

¼ cup (50 g) sugar

1 cinnamon stick (recommended, but optional)

I use every apple for applesauce—the bruised ones, the fat, shiny ones, and the ones that no one has chosen. I clean the kitchen of stray apples. But my favorites are the smaller, gnarly apples. Like a good bouillabaisse, the strongest, most interesting tastes seem to come from less obvious sources. When you find a good bunch, you will know it. The applesauce will taste, odd as it sounds, of apple, and the color may be slightly pink or even champagne.

I will serve it with a layer of Greek yogurt beneath it, or warmed with fresh whipped cream on top of it, or simply plain, with roasted walnuts or granola at the side. The trick, I think, is simply to make it.

Heat a medium or large saucepan, depending on the size and amount of apples, over medium heat. Add the butter. When it has melted, add the apples, salt, sugar, cinnamon stick (if using), and ¼ cup (60 ml) warm water. Stir to combine, then cover the pan and cook for 2 to 3 minutes. Remove the lid to check on things—you need the water to begin boiling and the steam to have built up. Stir again and turn the heat down a little. You want a rolling process, not a fury. Set the lid askew on top, but keep an eye on things. You want the apples to soften, but you do not want the moisture to boil away, and you definitely do not want anything to burn. Add 1 or 2 tablespoons of water if need be.

Poke the apples with a fork. When they are soft but before they turn to mush, turn off the heat and let them rest and cool. Spoon the cooked apples into a separate pan, discard the cinnamon stick, and put the food mill right on top of the saucepan they were cooked in. Pass the apples through the food mill, in batches, if necessary. Make certain to use a spatula to capture any sauce on the underside of the food mill.

Taste the applesauce; it may need a touch of salt or sugar or both. Store in clean glass jars with good lids. It should keep well in the refrigerator for 6 to 10 days. But first, eat some before it has chilled. Serve it in clear, low drinking glasses so one can see the flesh.

AVOCADO

The lovely avocado—also called the avocado pear, butter fruit, and the alligator pear—originated in Mexico. There are archeological references to it that date back to 10,000 BCE. Slowly, it began showing up in Central and South America (5000 BCE) and by 1500 CE, it had appeared in Europe and then South Africa and Australia. The migrating avocado.

It was not an important fruit in the United States until the start of the twentieth century, when its production was first introduced in Southern California. California did what it does best: It pounced and cultivated and developed. The very strain of avocado named Hass, with its black pebbled skin and medium size, was patented in 1935 by Rudy Hass, a postman and amateur horticulturalist in Southern California. Today, more than 80 percent of the world's avocados are the Hass variety. Avocados are now the official fruit of California, and 95 percent of all avocados sold in the United States are from California.

An avocado is a semitropical fruit, needing sun and humidity. It has no tolerance for frost and little for salty air, and in the right conditions, it can be harvested year-round. It is a treat on a tree.

For years, the avocado has implied a touch of Latin exoticism and a certain health food elitism, but it is surely loosed now. The production is so worldwide and capable that you can buy an avocado in the food mart of a mountain ski lodge. It is an integral part of fast food fare and health-food milkshakes and even high school menus.

Avocado Spread

2 ripe (not mushy)
  avocados, halved and
  pitted

1 juicy lime, quartered

Sea salt

1 garlic clove, minced
  or mashed

Pinch of red pepper
  flakes or tiny slices
  of fresh hot chile

Fresh ground black
  pepper

4 to 6 tortillas, pitas
  (see page 54), or
  slices of bread

2 tablespoons extra-
  virgin olive oil

¼ cup (10 g) chopped
  fresh cilantro

SERVES 4 TO 6 AS AN APPETIZER

We have used an avocado as a natural cup to hold a seafood marinara. We have folded avocado slices into cooked rice or lentils. We have softened the charge of a hamburger with avocado slices and lime juice. But most often, we serve it as a spread on tortillas, pita bread, or toast.

Scoop the avocado flesh into a medium bowl. Add a little lime juice and some salt. With a large fork, or even a potato masher, gently mash the avocados. You are not trying to make a smooth batter, so keep some lumps. Add the garlic, red pepper flakes, a good squeeze of lime, and salt and black pepper. Mix with a rubber spatula, two or three turns only.

Heat the tortillas in a cast-iron pan, on a pizza stone, or a griddle for just 1 minute. With a fork, spread the mixed avocado all over the tortillas. Add some salt and black pepper and lime and chop the tortillas into smaller assorted slices. Dash a few lines of olive oil across the slices, sprinkle the cilantro over the lot, and serve.

LEMONS AND LIMES

Ten years ago, I would not have written about lemons and limes. But they are now so much a part of my cooking that it would be incorrect not to mention them. I think there is never a meal that I do not use at least a touch of one or the other or both.

I use them, as most people do, for freshness and spirit—for their brightness of taste. They are the very front edge of present tense. Many times, I will simply rinse my hands with the juice of a lemon or lime, sure somehow that they will be cleansed and revived and refreshed.

When I am getting ready to cook, when I am getting the right knives and cutting board, salts and pepper, dishtowels and small bowls, there at the front I want at least a lemon and a lime. And I want them to be good ones. I made a birthday dinner at a friend's apartment in Manhattan one fall and needed everyone to help with the supplies. We had twelve avocados, ready to serve, and there were two netted bags of lovely small green limes, a dozen in each bag, and remarkably, there was not a tablespoon of lime juice that we could rescue from all the limes together. Never trust a netted bag of limes.

I have squeezed a lemon over carrots and celery, over chicken and halibut, over rib eye and Italian sausage, over mashed potatoes and stuffing, over raspberries and pears, over mushrooms and capocollo. It is the perfect spritz; the freshener, the light push to get on out there.

I have done the same with a lime, squeezing it on yogurt and lettuce, on corn and sprouts, on avocado and endive, on chicken and raw fish. Lime is slightly the odder one than lemon—a little stronger, a little quirkier and aromatic, a little more a favorite to fruits, to melons and squash and spice than the more genial lemon.

Meyer Lemon Dressing

Zest of 1 Meyer lemon

1 tablespoon fresh
Meyer lemon juice

1 tablespoon good
white wine vinegar

Sea salt

¼ cup (60 ml) extra-
virgin olive oil

1 tablespoon heavy
cream

Fresh cracked black
pepper

MAKES ABOUT ½ CUP (120 ML)

The Meyer lemon was imported from Asia at the start of the twentieth century and has become the gifted lemon to the new cuisine world. The Meyer lemon seems almost a cousin to a mandarin orange. It has a wonderful aromatic smell and the juice is not quite so acidic as that of a common lemon. Use this on fresh butter lettuce, which can stand up to a little coating, or on bitter greens like endive or radicchio, but use less than with the butter lettuce. Dress the salad in two stages. Use only half the dressing at first, and then judge how much more you might need once you see how all the parts are getting along. The dressing should be a complement, and a compliment, not a heavy sweater.

In a small bowl, stir together the lemon zest, lemon juice, vinegar, and a pinch of salt. Let it stand for a minute and then slowly whisk in the olive oil until combined. Whisk in the cream, crack in some fresh pepper, and taste, both for seasoning and texture. Add more salt if need be, and whisk in 1 teaspoon of cold water if it seems too thick. You can store it in an airtight jar in the refrigerator for at least a week.

VEGETABLES
From Side Dish to Main Course

The vegetable has outlasted its grumpy opponents. It has survived being overcooked, oversauced, and poorly produced. It is often the main course of a dinner—the very subtleties of cooking have rescued the vegetable.

This chapter includes my favorite preparations of my favorite vegetables. They are appetizers, side dishes, main courses, and even garnishes, but they always make the meal.

There is one thing you must keep in mind when preparing vegetables: At the very last moment, you want it to taste like that vegetable. It may involve particular preparations, but that is your precise goal, obvious as it seems. You may need a touch of vinegar or a pinch of salt; you may need to cook it a moment longer or a moment less. Sometimes, it may even be that the vegetable simply has little taste, and then you must repair in other ways—a sauce, a touch of butter, or an herb.

You will smell when a vegetable is ready, and you must move quickly. Trust your senses. Never has the vegetable been more important—it is now obvious that any sustainable food plan is literally linked to vegetables.

FIVE WAYS TO COOK

Asparagus

It is easier now to love asparagus than it used to be, but more difficult to buy good-quality asparagus. It is in every market, it seems, for nearly every month of the year. It is, like the avocado, a regular sight on the grocery shelves.

Avocados grow throughout the year, in temperate climates. But asparagus does not—its season is only two to three months long, in the belly of springtime. You must buy it with care and with common sense.

There is now, like salmon, a great demand for the earliest, freshest asparagus; it is the first brilliant vegetable to emerge out of the winter, a green stalk sticking straight up through the warmed soil—the hyacinth of the vegetables. The first local asparagus is expensive because it is the first; it has been rushed to market to signal the coming season. Celebrate it.

Asparagus is a sturdy sort. It can be packed to travel very long distances, even country to country. But no matter the brilliances of technology and travel, no asparagus can match a 6-inch (15-cm) bundle of stalks that has been picked that day. Asparagus is like that; it loves being local.

The first asparagus is naturally the thinnest. Cook it quickly and hot to preserve its youth. For any asparagus, I will soak it first in cold water for 3 to 5 minutes, to refresh it and to help it cook faster. As asparagus matures, you must peel the outside of the last 2 to 3 inches (5 to 7.5 cm) of stalk before you soak it or cook it.

The asparagus season will end in just two or three months, but there will still be asparagus on the stands. Groceries will have asparagus year-round. As I said, it is a sturdy sort, and, like the apple, it can be reasonably well held in suspension.

My advice is to move on to other vegetables, like the broccoli and cauliflower, which love the hot summer. The true, local asparagus will be back, but not until next year.

Here are some recipes for the celebration of the asparagus. Enjoy its arrival—you are in good company: There are references to steaming asparagus in Egyptian texts dated to 3000 BCE.

Asparagus with Parmesan and Arugula

12 to 16 medium asparagus
spears

1 teaspoon red wine vinegar

Sea salt

1 garlic clove, minced

2 tablespoons extra-virgin
olive oil

¼ pound (115 g) Parmigiano-
Reggiano cheese, some grated
and some in slices

1 lemon wedge

1 cup (20 g) arugula, washed and
spun dry

Fresh ground black pepper

SERVES 4

I have wonderful asparagus memories. It is the nature of its season. The asparagus arrives, usually in early April, in great abundance. By the start of June, it is gone. You will still see it at the grocery, but not in the farmers' markets. When it is fresh, and local, it dominates the options of what to cook. I always serve it with the arugula that has also just returned and a young Parmesan cheese. It seems to fit with both of them. When the asparagus is just right, you remember it. Make this wonderful dish with a light touch.

First, trim the asparagus, cutting 1 or 2 inches (2.5 or 5 cm) off the woody ends. With a swivel peeler, shave the bottom 3 to 4 inches (7.5 to 10 cm) of the stalks, taking off the harder outer skin. As you work, set the peeled asparagus in a shallow dish filled with cold water. Soak it for 5 minutes, then drain. (This seems to rehydrate the asparagus and help it cook more quickly.)

Meanwhile, make a vinaigrette: In a small glass bowl, combine the vinegar and a good pinch of salt. After a minute, add the garlic and whisk in the olive oil and a few drops of water. It should thicken and smooth a little. Set it aside.

In a pan large enough to hold the asparagus lying flat, heat 2 inches (5 cm) of water over high heat. When the water comes to a boil, add a good pinch of salt, then add the asparagus and put a lid on the pan. Allow the water to return to a boil, then turn the heat down to medium-low to maintain a gentle boil. The asparagus should be done in 3 to 4 minutes, when they are slightly softened but still firm. If it is the very skinny early asparagus, it will be done in 1 minute. Better to be early—you do not want stringy, overcooked asparagus, and that can mean no more than 30 seconds too long. If you smell asparagus, you are at the edge of too long. Get them out quickly and drain them well.

Lay the asparagus on a warmed platter. Sprinkle them with some sea salt, some grated Parmesan, and a little lemon juice. Lay the arugula on top, add the vinaigrette and the shaved Parmesan, and finish with a couple grindings of black pepper.

Asparagus, Grilled

1 tablespoon whole black peppercorns

1 pound (455 g) asparagus, trimmed, peeled, and soaked (see page 78)

2 tablespoons extra-virgin olive oil

Sea salt and fresh ground black pepper

1 teaspoon balsamic vinegar (optional)

SERVES 4

This is a fine way to cook and serve asparagus, if the asparagus is fresh and a grill is handy. The simple combination of the fresh asparagus and the direct heat from the fire seems to create a perfect taste. (But it will not work at all when the asparagus is out of season.)

Make certain the grill has been brushed clean, then heat it to its hottest temperature.

Crack the peppercorns in a pepper mill set to the coarsest grind or use a mortar and pestle. You want them very coarsely cracked.

Warm a wide glass or ceramic platter. Heat a small cast-iron skillet over medium heat. Put the cracked peppercorns into it and toast them for 2 to 3 minutes, then set the pan nearby. (Heating the peppercorns brings out their fire, and they look wonderful scattered around the asparagus.)

Set the asparagus in a shallow pan and pour 1 tablespoon of the olive oil over them, flipping the spears so they are coated on all sides with the oil. Salt them well, adding a couple grinds of pepper from the mill.

Using a cloth or a wad of paper towels held with tongs, swipe some olive oil from the roasting pan and rub it on the grill grates. Lay the asparagus across the grill, near but not on the center of the heat. With a spatula and tongs, turn the spears after 1 minute, then again after 30 seconds, and then again 30 seconds later.

The asparagus should have slight char marks and show some shrinking, but still be near firm. Lay the spears on the warmed platter and drizzle with the remaining 1 tablespoon olive oil. Immediately dot the spears with the vinegar, if using. Finish with the toasted cracked peppercorns and a touch more salt.

Skinny Asparagus with Tomatoes and Hot Pepper

1 pound (455 g) skinny asparagus, trimmed, soaked, and drained (see page 78)

2 tablespoons extra-virgin olive oil

3 tablespoons cold, unsalted butter

1 shallot or 2 spring onions, finely chopped

1 small dried red chile

1 garlic clove, thinly sliced

Sea salt and fresh ground black pepper

6 to 8 cherry tomatoes

¼ cup (60 ml) chicken stock, at a simmer

¼ cup (10 g) chopped fresh cilantro or basil leaves

SERVES 4

At the very start of the spring season, you can get fresh, skinny asparagus, and you can cook it with a particular, sprightly abandon. Once the asparagus matures, you can still make the dish, but it will not have the same flourish as in the early first days. The same, of course, is true of spring garlic, or the first wild mushrooms, or the early beans and peas.

Heat a big pot of water to a boil and toss the asparagus in. When the water comes back to a boil, quickly pull out and drain the asparagus.

Heat a wide sauté pan over medium-high heat for a minute. Add the olive oil, half the butter, and the shallot. After a minute, crush the dried red pepper into the pan and add the garlic. Toss and stir so the parts mix, then throw in the asparagus. Cook for no more than 3 minutes. The sauté cycle is a flash of exuberance for the first of the asparagus. You must shake the pan vigorously to get the asparagus to touch all the other elements. Add a good pinch of salt and black pepper. Throw in the tomatoes and stock and shake the pan even more, above the heat, to get the parts in contact. The stock will loosen and deglaze the pan's contents, and the tomatoes will create even more disorder as they split and leak.

Add the last of the butter, swirl for a second, then lay the asparagus in a jumble on a warmed platter. Sprinkle with the cilantro and give one last grind of black pepper.

Asparagus, Ham, and Peas with Penne Pasta

Sea salt

½ pound (225 g) asparagus, trimmed, peeled, soaked, and drained (see page 78)

¼ pound (115 g) sliced prosciutto

½ pound (225 g) good-quality dried penne pasta (or fusilli or orecchiette, shapes that like sauce and peas)

2 tablespoons extra-virgin olive oil

1 shallot, finely chopped

4 or 5 morel mushrooms (optional)

1 garlic clove, minced

1 tablespoon unsalted butter

Fresh ground black pepper

½ cup (70 g) fresh or frozen peas

½ cup (120 ml) heavy cream

¼ cup (13 g) chopped fresh flat-leaf parsley

½ cup (50 g) freshly grated Parmigiano-Reggiano cheese

2 or 3 fresh mint leaves (optional, if not using morels)

SERVES 4

You can easily link the asparagus into a chorus of parts and make a lovely dinner. This one uses a few pans, but then the parts all meet up and come out together.

Fill a large pot with water and bring it to a boil over high heat. When the water comes to a boil, add a good pinch of salt.

In a pan large enough to hold the asparagus lying flat, heat about 2 inches (5 cm) of water over high heat. When the water comes to a boil, add a good pinch of salt and the asparagus. Allow the water to return to a boil, then turn the heat down to medium-low to maintain a gentle boil. Put a lid on the pan and cook the asparagus for 3 minutes, until slightly softened but still very firm. Drain well. Cut the tips off the asparagus and set aside. Cut the stalks on a slight angle into ½-inch (12-mm) lengths and set them aside separately.

On a cutting board, stack the prosciutto slices lightly on top of one another and then roll up the stack like a sleeping bag. With a sharp knife, cut across the roll as thinly as possible. You should end up with a light jumble of prosciutto strips.

Add the pasta to the pot of boiling water and stir—make certain nothing is sticking. You should now have about 12 minutes to get the sauce ready to meet up with the pasta.

Heat a large sauté pan over medium heat. Add the olive oil and shallot and let them cook for 2 minutes. (If you are using morels, cut them in half and add them now.) Add the asparagus stalks and the garlic, and stir to combine. Cook, stirring and adding a little of the pasta water if the pan seems to be drying out too much.

In a smaller sauté pan, melt the butter over medium-low heat. Add the strips of prosciutto, a little salt, and a little pepper. They only need to cook for about 2 minutes, until they stiffen a little. Set the pan aside.

When the pasta has cooked for about 6 minutes, add the peas to the pot.

When the pasta is 2 minutes from being done, add most of the cream (see Note) to the pan with the asparagus stalks and stir to combine.

If the pan is too hot and the cream is bubbling too fast, turn the heat down a bit, but do not stop the momentum. Toss a little parsley into the mix.

Moments before the pasta is done, add the asparagus tips to the pasta pot, then drain it quickly, reserving some of the pasta cooking water just in case. The pasta mixture, still dripping wet, goes immediately into the pan with the cream sauce. Stir the pasta and peas and asparagus tips into the sauce.

The mixture will need salt and a couple fresh grinds of pepper, perhaps some pasta water and one-third of the grated cheese—it will melt both onto the pasta and into the sauce. Keep the sauce as thin as a gravy but not as thin as milk. If you have a few mint leaves, chop them thinly and add them (but not if you already added the morels).

Quickly portion the pasta into warm bowls, adding some more grated cheese, parsley, and pepper. Spoon some sauce around the rim of each bowl and then add the strands of prosciutto. They will bring their salty taste and slight crisp texture.

NOTE: Any leftover cream will help if you have held back some pasta or if you find you need a little more sauce. Just add it to the pan you heated the prosciutto in, thinning it a little with pasta water and bring to a gentle bubble. Crack some pepper in there, and sprinkle with some parsley, and use it as a kind of back up, if someone shows up late.

Asparagus and the Risotto

6 cups (1.4 L) homemade chicken or vegetable stock (see pages 35 to 36)

Sea salt

¾ pound (340 g) asparagus, trimmed, peeled, soaked, and drained (see page 78)

2 tablespoons extra-virgin olive oil

4 tablespoons (½ stick/55 g) cold, unsalted butter

1 medium yellow onion, finely chopped

1½ cups (285 g) imported Italian risotto rice (Arborio and vialone nano are favorites)

½ cup (120 ml) dry white wine

½ cup (50 g) freshly grated Parmigiano-Reggiano

Fresh ground black pepper

1 tablespoon finely chopped fresh flat-leaf parsley

SERVES 4

It is a good challenge to make a risotto with asparagus. Risotto represents a process, while asparagus represents a moment; risotto covers, and asparagus stands out. You must accommodate both.

Choose fresh, firm, and at least medium-thick asparagus. You could make it with very thin, early asparagus, but then you must stay nimble and light-handed so the oncoming rice does not trample the thin spears. You are contrasting the pale yellow of the rice, butter, and Parmesan with the bright green of the asparagus. Both risotto and asparagus must arrive at the finished plate looking their very best. Your allies are your ingredients—you will need a particularly good stock, Parmigiano-Reggiano, sea salt, parsley, and nearly all your attention.

In a saucepan, bring the stock to a simmer.

In a pan large enough to hold the asparagus lying flat, heat about 2 inches (5 cm) of water over high heat. When the water comes to a boil, add a good pinch of salt and the asparagus. Allow the water to return to a boil, then turn the heat down to medium-low to maintain a gentle boil. Put a lid on the pan and cook the asparagus for 3 minutes, until slightly softened but still firm. (If you are using the very thin asparagus, cook it for 1 minute only, and then pull it out.) Drain well, pouring the asparagus cooking water into the pan with the stock. Cut the tips from the asparagus and set them aside. Cut the stalks on an angle into ½-inch (12-mm) pieces. If they are quite thick, cut them in half lengthwise as well. They will cook with the rice, so they should not be left chunky. Set them aside separately.

Heat a heavy-bottomed pan over medium to medium-high heat. Add 1 tablespoon of the olive oil, 2 tablespoons of the butter, and the onion. Cook, stirring well and often, until the onion begins to pale, about 5 minutes. Add the asparagus stalks, stirring to mix. A minute later, add the rice. Stir and stir—you are toasting the rice, but only for a minute or so.

Add the wine. It will sizzle and bubble and, in a minute or two, evaporate. You are by now stirring without interruption. Add two ladles of the stock, then stir. Check the heat level under the pan. Risotto comes together only on the knife-edge between too hot and not hot enough. If the pan is too hot, the stock will not have time to be absorbed by the rice. If it is not hot enough, the rice will soak and drown in the stock.

You must find the right temperature; the place between pushing uphill and running downhill. The pace must be rapid, it must not be frantic, and it cannot be languid.

Continue to add stock, one or two ladles at a time, and stir near continuously for about 18 minutes, while the risotto gets slightly heavier as it absorbs the liquid and expands. As time passes, you must be careful to stir deeply and not let any surface burn or get too dry. Each moment that the rice begins to dry out and stick, add more stock. (You may not use all the stock—I try to always have some left over, to refresh the asparagus tips later or to moisten the rice if it must sit for long.)

Taste the rice at 18 minutes—it should be tender, but still have the slightest bite. If it is too firm, cook for another minute or so, stirring and adding a little more stock.

Remarkably, for a process that has been sustained for 18 to 20 minutes, there is a moment when the risotto is precisely done. Turn off the heat beneath the pan, cover, and let it rest for a minute.

Add the asparagus tips to the stock for just a minute to warm and revive them or sprinkle some hot water over the tips. Remove them with a slotted spoon and give them a little salt.

Quickly and firmly stir the remaining 2 tablespoons butter into the risotto so it melts and becomes incorporated, then add most of the cheese. The risotto is at its heaviest, so stir deeply and well—it should not be soupy, nor should it feel like a lump. You can thin it slightly with a little stock or thicken it slightly with a moment over low heat. Taste and adjust the seasoning.

Serve the risotto in warm bowls, with the asparagus tips laid on top. Sprinkle with some of the cheese, pepper, and the parsley, and drizzle a thin line of the remaining olive oil over the top of each dish.

FIVE WAYS TO COOK

Broccoli

You must come to terms with broccoli. It has wonderful versatility, it is available year-round in good variety, it can carry nearly an entire meal, and it can be prepared quickly. That said, it can be a tricky partner to meals. It comes from the *Brassica* genus—cabbage and such—so you must be careful to not overcook it, or the sulfurous smell will cut into your anticipation.

In culinary terms, it has the perfect lineage, having been first perfected in Italy two thousand years ago. It was not popular in America until nearly the 1930s, and in the 1950s, it was put on its own kind of blacklist, as it became typical to boil it for thirty minutes. With the lid on. My mother was a gentle and intuitive cook, but she was a butcher of broccoli.

In recent times, broccoli has been rescued by two factors: One, there was a medical discovery that broccoli had distinct anti-cancer, anti-bacterial properties. And two, Italian cuisine became extraordinarily popular, and the Italians know well and naturally how to cook broccoli. They blanch it, but only for a minute or two (after five minutes of boiling, it quickly begins to lose its curative strengths). If you should be fortunate enough to travel to Italy, note how they cook and use broccoli—it will never, ever, have a sour taste or smell.

There are a couple of important details to preparing it. First, you must soak it in cold water. That will restore and refresh it, but will also drown any critters who have curled up in it—cutworms and such. They are rare in supermarket broccoli, but common in the organic type, of course, and especially in the farmers' market variety. Always soak it. Trim it just before soaking, either just the ends, or you could cut it into parts. Five minutes of soaking in cold water is certainly enough. Should there be a slight film to the soaking water or debris in the bowl, change the water a time or two until it is clearer.

Broccoli has a long, thick stem that is probably the tastiest part, but the part most often thrown away. Peel away the outer length, using a peeler or small knife, and it will cook better.

If blanching or slightly boiling, always add salt to the water after it comes to a boil, then drop in the broccoli, and of course only boil it until it slightly softens—with fresh broccoli that might mean only three minutes or so. If you can smell the broccoli, that is your warning that it is done or near so. You must drain it before it has completely softened. It is a task of vigilance to not overcook it.

Ninety percent of the broccoli you will buy is near precisely the same. You might find some in a lonely all-night mart that appear particularly pale, but for the most part, it seems the green version of the yellow onion. But it does indeed have its natural season, late spring to middle summer, and for that period, you can use it with even more exuberance.

Broccoli with Garlic, Oil, and Hot Pepper

1 pound (455 g) broccoli

Sea salt

¼ cup (60 ml) extra-virgin
    olive oil

2 garlic cloves, finely chopped

Pinch of red pepper flakes

¼ cup (13 g) chopped fresh
    flat-leaf parsley

Fresh cracked black pepper

SERVES 4

Start here to learn the dance steps with broccoli. It is first blanched in salted water, then quickly sautéed with garlic in olive oil—all very simple. But it must be done with some precision—even a slightly neglected piece of broccoli can turn sullen. If the broccoli is fresh and you have been vigilant not to overcook it, then you can serve this all by itself. And people will talk about your broccoli.

Trim the dried end of the broccoli stalk and peel the outer skin from it. Split the broccoli into lengths, each with a floret on the end of the stalk. As you work, drop the broccoli into a large bowl of cool water. Soak it for 5 minutes.

Bring a big pot of water to a boil. Add 1 tablespoon of salt. Drop the broccoli into the water and cook until you can pierce the stalk with a fork. If it is very fresh, it might be done in 3 minutes. Drain it quickly.

Set a sauté pan over medium heat. Add the olive oil and garlic right away and heat so the garlic takes on some color but does not burn.

The moment you smell the garlic, add the broccoli pieces and red pepper flakes. Season with salt and add the parsley. Turn all the pieces several times to coat them with the oil, then transfer the broccoli to a warmed plate.

Pour the oil from the pan over the broccoli and crack some black pepper over the top. Taste and adjust the seasoning, and serve immediately.

Broccoli Fair with Butter and Parmesan Cheese

1 pound (455 g) broccoli

Sea salt

5 tablespoons (70 g) cold, unsalted butter

½ cup (50 g) freshly grated Parmigiano-Reggiano cheese

SERVES 4

It is a moment's sleight of hand, adding broccoli to sweet butter and cheese. By nature, the broccoli would stay more to the grumpy side. You must work quickly. When broccoli begins to cool, it starts thinking about being grumpy again. Make certain the serving dish and plates are warm.

Trim the dried end of the broccoli stalk and peel the outer skin from it. Soak the broccoli in a large bowl of cool water for 5 minutes.

Bring a big pot of water to a boil. Add 1 tablespoon of salt. Drop the broccoli into the water and cook until you can pierce the stalk with a fork. If it is very fresh, it might be done in 3 minutes. Drain it quickly.

Shake the water off the broccoli. Cut the crown from the stalk and separate the florets. Halve the stalk lengthwise and cut it into 1-inch (2.5-cm) lengths.

Heat a large skillet over medium-high heat. You want the pan to be hot enough to briskly cook the broccoli, but not burn the butter. Add the butter and as soon as it foams, add the broccoli and shake well to coat all the pieces. Add a good pinch of salt and shake well.

The broccoli will heat in the pan for only 2 minutes. Add half the cheese and stir to combine.

Transfer the broccoli to a warmed plate or shallow bowl and top with the remaining cheese. Season with salt and serve, pronto!

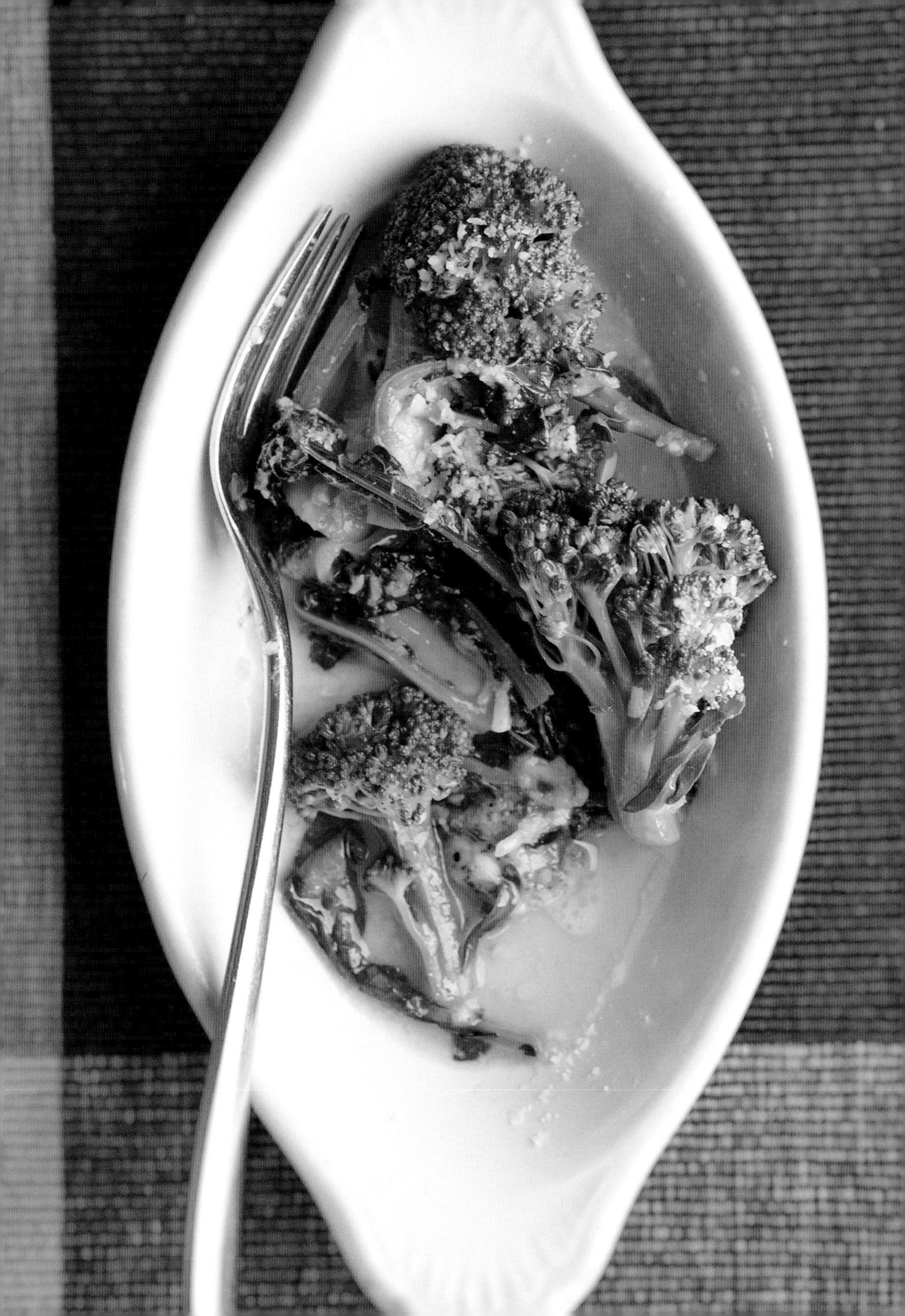

Broccoli Tango with Garlic, Ginger, Shallot, Spice, and Soy

½ pound (225 g) broccoli

Sea salt

¼ pound (115 g) whole sunchokes (Jerusalem artichokes)

¼ cup (60 ml) extra-virgin olive oil

1 shallot, quartered and thinly sliced

2-inch (5-cm) piece fresh ginger, peeled and finely chopped

2 garlic cloves, finely chopped

1 hot red chile, thinly sliced

½ teaspoon sesame oil

2 tablespoons soy sauce

½ cup (30 g) chopped scallion greens

SERVES 4

This is a night on the town for the broccoli, the quick exuberance of tastes and heat. It is a recipe well suited to adaptation; you can certainly add wild mushrooms and peppers, peas and asparagus tips and bits of green, whatever is on hand. But let them be additions that will keep the velocity—it is not a dish for softer vegetables or slower dance steps.

I have served this broccoli by itself, but also with steamed rice. And some nights, I have cooked a pasta like orecchiette and added it, still wet, to the pan; the starch from the pasta thickens the sauce. If you do want to add pasta, then do not use the sesame oil and the soy sauce and add grated Parmesan instead.

Trim the dried end of the broccoli stalk and peel the outer skin from it. Soak the broccoli in a large bowl of cool water for 5 minutes.

Bring a big pot of water to a boil. Add 1 tablespoon of salt. Drop the broccoli and whole sunchokes into the boiling water and cook for 3 minutes. Drain them quickly.

Shake the water off the broccoli. Cut the crown from the stalk and separate the florets, keeping them no more than 1 inch (2.5 cm) big. Cut the stalk into thin, pencil-like strips. Peel and thinly slice the sunchokes.

Heat a sauté pan over medium-high heat. Add the olive oil and the shallot and stir. Cook for a minute, then add the ginger and garlic and stir. Before the garlic can burn, add the chile and the broccoli and mix it all well. Throw in some salt and the sunchokes and toss to get everything moving.

When the broccoli and sunchokes begin to brown slightly, after 2 to 3 minutes, turn the heat down a notch. Add the sesame oil and then the soy sauce. It should bubble with the heat. Carefully mix and spoon the broccoli onto warmed plates. Sprinkle with the scallions to finish.

VARIATION: If you wish, you can deglaze the pan with some hot water or hot chicken stock, add a little tomato paste or cold butter to thicken it, and when it has reduced, drizzle it over the broccoli. It is a handy variation if you need a gravy to tie things together or a sauce to bring more flavor. When broccoli is at its best, it does not need much help.

Broccoli for the Day with Hummus and Lentils

½ pound (225 g) broccoli

Sea salt

¼ cup (60 ml) extra-virgin
olive oil

2 garlic cloves, minced

6 to 8 seeds from a small, hot,
dried chile

2 tablespoons cooked lentils
(see page 236); cooked
cannellini or kidney beans
(see page 234); or cooked
quinoa (see page 237),
at room temperature

¼ cup (60 ml) hummus

1 tablespoon chopped fresh flat-
leaf parsley

4 or 5 fresh mint leaves, chopped
(optional)

Fresh cracked black pepper

SERVES 4

**A good vegetable can be enough all on its own, but you could add a
piece of fish, lamb, or chicken for a broader meal. Or put a spoonful
of salted Greek yogurt alongside the broccoli, and let the olive oil just
run over the yogurt. Some days, frankly, that seems plenty to me.**

**It is an interesting dish. You should taste the garlic, of course, but also
the hot pepper, the olive oil, and the good salt and freshly cracked
pepper—they combine to make it all lively. The hummus is a smooth
luxury, and the lentils keep it all grounded. If made with a light touch
and some tempo, it can seem quite a piece, especially in light of its
simple structure.**

Trim the dried end of the broccoli stalk and peel the outer skin from it.
Soak the broccoli in a large bowl of cool water for 5 minutes.

Bring a big pot of water to a boil. Add 1 tablespoon of salt. Drop the
broccoli into the boiling water and cook for 3 minutes. Drain it quickly.
Chop the broccoli stalk and florets into 1-inch (2.5-cm) pieces and give
them a sprinkle of salt.

Heat a 10-inch (25-cm) sauté pan over medium heat for a moment,
then add half the olive oil, the garlic, and the hot red pepper seeds,
and stir together. After a minute, as the garlic starts to smell, add the
chopped broccoli and stir well to mix. If it seems too dry, add a bit
more olive oil. You are not frying the broccoli, but it is not lying in the
sun, either—keep it moving.

After 2 to 3 minutes, taste a piece. It should be hot and nearly ready.
Add the lentils and a pinch of salt, stir well, and cook for a minute to
refresh and introduce the lentils. Scrape the mixture onto a warmed
plate, wipe out the pan with a paper towel, and return it to the stove
over low heat.

Add a little more of the olive oil to the pan and heat for 10 seconds.
Add the hummus, warming it in the olive oil. Stir the hummus, add 1
teaspoon of warm water to thin it slightly, and stir to combine it like
a gravy. Using a rubber spatula, lay the softened hummus across the
broccoli like a shawl, with some of it free on the plate.

Garnish with the parsley (and mint, if using), season with some salt and
cracked black pepper, and drizzle with the rest of the olive oil.

Broccoli and Spanish Ham, Wrapped in Spaghetti

¾ pound (340 g) broccoli

Sea salt

¼ pound (115 g) serrano ham, cut into thin strips

2 tablespoons cold, unsalted butter

¼ pound (115 g) good-quality dried spaghetti (see Note)

¼ cup (60 ml) extra-virgin olive oil, plus more as needed

3 garlic cloves, crushed a little

Pinch of red pepper flakes

Fresh ground black pepper

½ cup (50 g) freshly grated Parmigiano-Reggiano cheese, plus more as needed

¼ cup (60 ml) heavy cream, at room temperature

SERVES 4

You can use any sort of dried ham for this, but I think the Spanish *jamón serrano* is the best. It is more intense than the Italian prosciutto—a little saltier. This is a dish for the slices of ham that did not get eaten the first day.

Trim the dried end of the broccoli stalk and peel the outer skin from it. Soak the broccoli in a large bowl of cold water for 5 minutes.

Bring a big pot of water to a boil. Add 1 tablespoon of salt. Drop the broccoli into the boiling water and cook for 3 minutes. Drain it quickly. Fill the pot with fresh water and bring it to a boil for the pasta. Chop the broccoli into 2- to 3-inch (5- to 7.5-cm) pieces. Drain them on a paper towel for a moment to remove any excess water.

Heat a medium saucepan over low heat. Add the butter. When it has melted, add the strips of ham, stir, and cook for 2 minutes, until the ham slightly crisps and the pieces stiffen and seem almost to stand up. Salt it a little, turn off the heat, and set it nearby.

Toss 1 tablespoon of salt into the boiling water, add the pasta, and stir. Cook the pasta for 12 minutes, or as directed on the package.

Heat a sauté pan over medium heat. Add the olive oil and garlic. You want the garlic to slightly color, both to flavor the oil and the broccoli. Add the red pepper flakes, the broccoli, a good pinch of salt, and a couple grinds of black pepper. Shake the pan well to mix. You are not lightly sautéing the broccoli—this is rougher treatment than that. If need be, add a little more olive oil.

Drain the pasta, reserving ¼ cup (60 ml) of the pasta cooking water, and add the pasta to the pan with the broccoli. Season with a little salt and mix it all well. Cook everything together for a minute, adding a little pasta water if the mixture appears dry. Remove the pan from the heat, add a little grated cheese, and stir to combine.

With tongs or a slotted spoon, transfer the strips of ham to a plate. Add the cream and 1 tablespoon of the pasta water to the butter remaining in the saucepan; stir and pour the mixture all over the broccoli and spaghetti. Quickly fold it all together.

Only then will you put the strips of ham all over the top, and add a little more cheese, salt, and black pepper. Serve immediately, with extra cheese on the table and perhaps a thin drizzle of olive oil across each serving.

FIVE WAYS TO COOK
Carrots

It is hard to find a good carrot. They are like a broom—just get me a broom. Of course, there are many varieties of broom and carrot, some quite wonderful, and some just showing up to do the job.

It is an easily influenced crop, pushed by fertilizers and accelerants and manipulation, and I get picky about the source of my carrots, preferring local varieties. I avoid the so-called baby carrots, those little bullets, not because they do not appear delectable, but because my son's two rabbits, who would eat the box a new radio came in, would not touch them.

The good thing about carrots is that you often do not even have to cook them. They are often best served raw. You will be tempted to use the first spring carrots in the simplest ways, splayed out to show that winter has passed. But the best raw carrots are later in the season, when they have had time to get all their fiber and taste. (Use the earliest ones in the oven, with herbs, roasts, and such.) Obviously, a carrot with its greens still attached seems fresher, and the greens actually do keep the carrot fresh longer.

When you do serve carrots raw, be generous with the company you give them. Have a small container of good flaky sea salt to the side, but also some hummus, chutney, lemon juice, chopped cilantro, and perhaps a little Greek yogurt with a sprinkle of Aleppo pepper.

The raw carrot, sliced into sticks and rinsed, is a fine, often forgotten, addition to airline travel, especially if you include a little hummus. They will seem like the only fresh thing on a long flight, they are quite easily digested, and they are good allies for passing time and musing. Let the raw carrot push you around to making sauces that you had forgotten— romesco, salmoriglio, anchovy, or spiced hummus. Every culture has independent sauces, to help with the tasks of color, taste, and attraction. They are the scarves and hats and blouses and even jewelry of a food culture. Let the carrot dip into all of them.

Here are five ways to use carrots, ways that I know will work. I am pleased, to tell the truth, to even have a list.

Sweet Carrots

1 pound (455 g) young carrots, halved lengthwise

3 tablespoons cold, unsalted butter

Sea salt

2 tablespoons brown sugar or pure maple syrup

SERVES 2 TO 4

Sometimes, when it is cold, or seems a time not fit for raw carrots, you can make sweet carrots. Cook them quickly, in a little butter and salt, and then add some brown sugar or maple syrup near the end.

Heat a sauté pan, large enough to hold the carrots in a single layer, over medium heat. Add the carrots, about ½ inch (12 mm) of water (or enough to get the carrots wet but not completely covered), the butter, and some salt. Let the water come to a light boil and then adjust the heat to keep it simmering. Stir a couple of times.

When the carrots have softened a little, in 2 to 3 minutes, add the brown sugar, stir again, and cook for a couple of minutes more. Do not let the sugar burn, but it should caramelize and brown the carrots a little. The water should be nearly gone, the carrots tender and sweet.

Turn the carrots out onto a warmed plate with their liquid, add some salt, and serve immediately.

Carrots Roasted with Herbs

1 pound (455 g) carrots

Sea salt

¼ cup (60 ml) extra-virgin olive oil, plus more for serving

Pinch of Aleppo pepper (pul biber) or cayenne

6 to 8 sprigs fresh thyme

Flaky sea salt and fresh cracked black pepper

SERVES 2 TO 4

If you serve these carrots to guests as hors d'oeuvres, you will get the empty plate right back. Roasted carrots love being a solo performer—people then will pay attention to the taste. They are, as well, a wonderful side dish to any main course. Use early carrots, if you can get them. I have an old roasting pan, blackened on its exterior, and roasting carrots—or bread crumbs, or bell peppers—is what keeps it employed.

Preheat the oven to 425°F (220°C).

Cut the carrots into 4- to 6-inch (10- to 15-cm) lengths and halve them lengthwise. Toss the carrots, a good pinch of sea salt, and the olive oil in a stainless-steel bowl. Add the Aleppo pepper. Turn out the carrots into a roasting pan and toss half the thyme on top.

Roast for 10 minutes, then give the pan a good shake so the carrots roll about. Ten minutes later, turn the oven temperature down to 300°F (150°C) and shake the pan again. Bake for 10 minutes more (for a total of 30 minutes), until the carrots are a little blackened and softened.

Pull them out of the oven and lay them willy-nilly on a white dinner plate, with a little extra olive oil, some cracked black pepper, the rest of the thyme, and a visible scattering of flaky sea salt.

Carrots and Mustard

Sea salt

2 to 3 pounds (910 g to 1.4 kg) carrots, thinly sliced (¼ inch/ 6 mm thick) on an angle

5 tablespoons (70 g) unsalted butter

½ teaspoon sugar

1 teaspoon all-purpose flour

½ tablespoon Dijon mustard

¼ cup (60 ml) chicken or vegetable stock, or pan juices from a roast

Fresh ground black pepper

1 cup (30 g) homemade croutons (see page 57; optional)

¼ cup (13 g) chopped fresh flat-leaf parsley

SERVES 4

If you have a good supply of fresh, young carrots and need something to accompany a roast, a chicken, or a lovely fish, this is an interesting way to get the carrots involved. Try to remember to add the croutons; they lend a separate texture and are a good partner with the sauce.

Bring a large pot of water to a boil. Add a good pinch of salt, then add the carrots and blanch for 2 minutes or so. Drain well.

Heat a heavy sauté pan over medium heat. Add 4 tablespoons (55 g) of the butter. When it has melted, add the carrots, 1 teaspoon salt, and the sugar, and stir it all to coat. Turn down the heat to low and cook, stirring often, for 8 minutes. Add ¼ cup (60 ml) warm or hot water. It should bubble a bit, reacting to the butter and sugar. Stir to loosen everything and cook until the water has nearly cooked away. Add the remaining 1 tablespoon butter and the flour and stir, as if you're making a gravy.

Add the Dijon mustard and stock, to finish the mustard sauce.

Taste and adjust the seasoning. Finish with a little pepper, and fold in the croutons (if using), and the parsley.

Carrots Browned and Sprinkled with Parmesan

1 pound (455 g) medium carrots, peeled and rinsed

Sea salt

2 tablespoons unsalted butter

1 tablespoon brown sugar

¼ cup (25 g) freshly grated Parmigiano-Reggiano cheese

SERVES 4

The carrots sweeten as they contract. The difficulty is typically making enough of them—they have a specific, wonderful taste. They can tie up one or two large pans and much of the stovetop, so dole them out judiciously.

Cut the carrots into ½-inch (12-mm)-thick rounds and lay them in a single layer in a sauté pan. You will likely need two pans.

Add ¼ inch (6 mm) of water, some salt, and the butter, and bring the water to a slow, steady boil over medium heat. Cook until they have softened but are not quite done, 12 minutes or so. This should use up a good bit of the water. Add the sugar and stir.

If there is more than the barest amount of water left, pour some off. Turn the heat down a little. Cook until browned on one side, then turn each carrot and brown on the second side, 10 minutes or so total. The carrots will shrink as they cook and the remaining liquid will cook off.

Add some salt and lay the carrots in a warmed serving bowl. Sprinkle with the cheese while they are still warm.

Pickled Carrots

1 tablespoon sea salt, plus more
as needed

1 teaspoon whole black
peppercorns

1 pound (455 g) medium carrots

½ cup (120 ml) red wine vinegar

½ cup (100 g) sugar

1 bay leaf

1 garlic clove

MAKES ABOUT 1 QUART (960 ML)

The carrot is the perfect vegetable for marinating, in terms of its color, texture, length, reputation, and availability. Marinate them while you are doing other things, for they simply need to be parboiled and then soaked in a brine with herbs for a couple of hours. They are perfect with sandwiches and salads, but sometimes I put them out as an appetizer before dinner.

Bring a large pot of water to a boil. Add a good pinch of salt.

Heat a small cast-iron skillet over medium heat. Toast the peppercorns for 2 to 3 minutes, then set the pan nearby.

Cut the carrots to 4-inch (10-cm) lengths, halving or quartering them lengthwise, depending on size. Drop them into the boiling water and cook for 10 minutes or so, until they are slightly more tender than firm. Drain them well. Let cool, then pack into 3 or 4 sterilized 6-ounce (170-g) glass jars.

In a saucepan, bring 3 cups (720 ml) water and the vinegar to a boil. Add the salt, sugar, bay leaf, garlic, and toasted peppercorns and simmer for couple of minutes. Let cool slightly.

Pour the pickling brine over the carrots, cover tightly, and let the flavor develop for at least a couple of hours before serving. Refrigerate the cooled jars. They will keep for a month.

FIVE WAYS TO COOK

Onions

It is easy enough to overlook the onion. It is available worldwide and in every season. The onion is a character actor, crucial to nearly every production. It is the base of many a soup and sauce, of every stew and roast, of every condiment and paste.

Every year, my neighbor Bob grows onions—red and yellow varieties—in long, loose-soiled rows, and by fall, his garage is filled with hundreds of softball-size onions, slowly drying. If I stop over at his garden in August, Bob will pull up five or six onions, shedding dirt, and hand them over to me. What always surprises me is that a six-month cycle, started back in the rains of March with Bob on his knees tapping in the seedlings, has ended so abruptly. Keep in mind the cycle of the onion—it will make it less a task when you are trying to get them chopped.

Bob knows I love cooking the onions before they have been dried. Get an outdoor grill started. Trim the tops of the fresh onions, leaving about 3 inches (7.5 cm) of the green leaves and peeling away the outer skin, but leave the roots; they will help hold the onion together while it cooks.

If the onions are at least as big as a baseball, halve them vertically, so both halves retain some root and some leaves. In a large bowl, coat them lightly in olive oil, add some salt and pepper, and lay them on the hot grill, cut side down. You will need to turn them three or four times and likely move them off the hottest part of the grill so they do not char too much, but they will be soft and slightly burnt in 4 to 5 minutes. Let them cool near the fire.

The onions will have sweetened from the heat, and their retained moisture will have kept them soft. You can also use spring onions, the half-grown youths, in the same way, searing them on the grill and rolling them about to heat each side. If using spring onions, it is not necessary to cut them; simply trim the leaves to within 3 inches (7.5 cm) of the body.

Once cooled a little, cut them into pieces, tossing any outer layers that might not be suitable. Put the pieces into a large bowl, add salt and pepper and more olive oil, and toss in anything else—grilled zucchini, cut tomatoes, basil, corn, blanched cauliflower, chives, mushrooms, bits of chicken or fish.

For one dinner I simply added the juice of two limes, the meat of two ripe avocados, and a pile of chopped cilantro and parsley to the grilled onions—it was a celebration.

If it isn't the season for grilling, there are so many other methods that showcase the many virtues of the trusty onion. To follow are some of my favorite ways to enjoy the allium.

Onions Sautéed with Peppercorns and Bay Leaf

2 tablespoons whole black peppercorns (I prefer Tellicherry)

¼ cup (60 ml) extra-virgin olive oil

1 pound (455 g) fresh yellow onions, cut into ⅛-inch (3-mm) slices

1 bay leaf

Sea salt

SERVES 4

There are many versions of this, and this one is simply a start. But it is a good one, which will lead you to try the hundreds of variations (for one, see the grilled onions described on page 113). It is not a condiment, nor an occasion to caramelize—it is a side dish. It celebrates the distinct heat of black pepper, the sweetness of the onion, and the slight bitterness of bay leaf. There is a lot going on for a moment. Serve the onions with seafood or pork, with rice, or with lentils.

Heat a sauté pan over medium heat. Very coarsely crush the peppercorns and toast them for 3 minutes. Add the olive oil, onions, and bay leaf. Stir to combine and cook, stirring often, for 15 minutes, until they are soft and have begun to merge. Season with salt and let cool. Toss the bay leaf—it has left its tone—and serve.

Roasted Onions, Thyme, and Carrots

6 spring onions, with leaves, or
  2 medium yellow onions

12 baby carrots, with greens

¼ cup (60 ml) extra-virgin olive
  oil, plus more for serving

Sea salt and fresh ground black
  pepper

6 sprigs fresh thyme

SERVES 4

There are really two perfect seasons for this recipe—the middle of spring, when the first young onions arrive, or later in summer, when the softball-size crop of yellow onions is pulled out to dry. They both work as a welcome accent to just about any meal. Serve them alongside anything from a roast chicken to guacamole.

Preheat the oven to 450°F (230°C).

Trim the onion leaves to 2 to 3 inches (5 to 7.5 cm) above the bulb. (If using yellow onions, slice them as thinly as possible.) Trim the carrot stems to 1 inch (2.5 cm).

In a large stainless-steel bowl, toss together the onions, carrots, and olive oil until the vegetables are well coated. Season well with salt and pepper, toss the mixture again, then spread the mixture in a single layer in a roasting pan. Toss the thyme on top.

Roast the vegetables for 10 minutes, then flip them and roast for 5 minutes more. They should be browned by then; if not, go a little longer. Then turn the oven temperature down to 250°F (120°C) and bake for 10 to 15 minutes more.

Add a little salt for their efforts and finish with a thin line of olive oil before serving.

Caramelized Onions

1 teaspoon walnut or canola oil

1½ pounds (680 g) yellow
onions, thinly sliced

1 tablespoon fine sugar

1 teaspoon sea salt

1 teaspoon fresh ground
black pepper

1 teaspoon balsamic vinegar

MAKES ABOUT ¾ CUP (170 G)

These are quite good and certainly easy to do, but I often forget about them. Then something, like a burger, comes up to remind me. Try them on tacos, or add a touch of the compote to the surface of a lentil soup, or string them alongside a salad. They are a perfect addition to any lunch or sandwich.

Heat a saucepan over medium heat for 20 seconds. Add the oil, and then the onions. Stir them well to coat and then add the sugar, salt, and pepper. Stir again and cover. Reduce the heat to low—you are sweating the onions, not browning them yet. Stir every 5 minutes. After 30 minutes, the onions should be soft and slightly separate. Uncover the pan and cook for 30 minutes more. The onions will begin to caramelize and brown. Stir them often to prevent burning.

Add the vinegar at the very end. Stir well to incorporate. Transfer the onions to a ceramic bowl with a lid. Keep them covered and let them rest until cool. They can be used once they have cooled. Refrigerate leftovers in an airtight container—they will keep at least a week.

Pickled Red Onions

1 pound (455 g) red onions,
    cut into ¼- to ½-inch
    (6- to 12-mm)-thick slices

2 cups (480 ml) apple
    cider vinegar

2 tablespoons sugar

Pinch of red pepper flakes

1 tablespoon sea salt

1 tablespoon whole black
    peppercorns

1 bay leaf

1 garlic clove

MAKES ABOUT 2 CUPS (480 ML)

Make these when you are distracted with other matters. It only takes a moment, but hours later, and for a month or so, you have these wonderful pieces of pickled onion—a better result than most distractions. Serve them with fish and pâté, with hamburgers and blue cheese, with tuna and salmon, and with rice.

Put the onions in a large bowl. In a separate large bowl, combine the remaining ingredients with 1 cup (240 ml) hot water and stir to dissolve the salt and sugar. Pour the brine over the onions. Let the mixture sit for 1 hour, then transfer the onions to clean glass jars with lids and fill to within ¼ inch (6 mm) of the top with the brining liquid. You can use them right away, but they do get better with a little age. Cover and refrigerate—they will keep for a couple of months.

Oven-Baked Onions, Tomatoes, and Potatoes with Romano Cheese

2 pounds (910 g) Yellow Finn or
  new potatoes, peeled and cut
  into ½-inch (12-mm) slices

2 cups (220 g) very thinly
  sliced yellow onions (2 or 3
  medium onions)

4 to 6 medium tomatoes, peeled,
  seeded, and chopped

1 cup (100 g) freshly grated
  Pecorino Romano

2 tablespoons fresh oregano
  leaves, or 1 tablespoon
  fresh thyme leaves plus 1
  tablespoon fresh sage leaves,
  lightly chopped

Sea salt and fresh ground black
  pepper

¼ cup (60 ml) extra-virgin
  olive oil

2 tablespoons unsalted butter,
  cut into cubes

SERVES 4 TO 6

Someone gave me a great chunk of Italian Pecorino Romano cheese—
five times more than I knew how to use. I knew to grate it on fresh
pesto, to mix it with Parmigiano-Reggiano, to expect its wonderful
pairing with rich meat sauces. It sticks up, the true Romano, no matter
how deep the sauce. But I had to go to the boss, Marcella Hazan, whose
Italian cookbooks have hand-carried so many out into cooking freedom,
to get the full context and to get a wider sense of cooking with it.

I followed every reference that Hazan made about Pecorino Romano,
determined to put my bounty of cheese to work. Soup, bruschetta,
slow-cooked beef—they all made a home for the cheese. But my favorite
is a great mix of tomatoes, onions, sliced potatoes, a full cup of freshly
grated Pecorino Romano, and a little oregano and olive oil—all roasted
together. Here is my version of it.

Preheat the oven to 400°F (205°C). Position a rack in the top third of
the oven.

Rinse the sliced potatoes, drain them for a moment, then put them, still
wet, into a big bowl. Add the onions, tomato, cheese, herbs, and salt
and pepper to taste. Mix well with clean hands.

Use a little olive oil to coat a large baking dish. Fill it with the potato
mixture. Pat it down a little, drizzle the rest of the olive oil around
the surface, and bury the pieces of the butter in it. Top with a last few
grinds of pepper.

Bake for 1 hour. Turn the potatoes a couple of times, so the browned
surfaces will be shared. When the potatoes are soft, it is done. It can sit
for 10 minutes or so while you get the rest of a meal in place.

FIVE WAYS TO COOK
Cauliflower

Like broccoli, cauliflower is also from the *Brassica* genus. They both share a very long history, with references from the Middle East that are dated from the fifth and sixth centuries BCE. In culinary terms, the earliest references are from Italy, about two thousand years ago. The Italians, of course, soon cultivated varieties of many colors—elegant greens, purples, and oranges.

But the most common variety is the white cauliflower. It is a sturdy sort, with a very firm head (if it is not hard, do not buy it), and you must keep in mind how often it gets handled. Wash it well in cold water before cooking it. Do not boil it for great lengths of time. In fact, longer boiling all but ruins its wonderful nutritional value, not to mention its reputation. It can be ready after four to five minutes of rolling around in boiling water. But it can also be steamed, roasted, deep-fried, and baked.

Cauliflower does not have the popularity broccoli enjoys in the United States. Perhaps, like broccoli, it is the memory of over boiling and a slight sulfurous smell that does it. I think, as well, that cauliflower has an exoticism to it, a privacy of being tightly bundled, and that has kept it slightly to the side of popularity.

Regardless, it is one of the most helpful vegetables to have on hand. It has the best sort of spirit. It loves joining into soups and salads and stir-fries. It loves butter and grated cheese and creams, but it is happy as well to dress up in the exotic outfits of spices and oils and very hot sautés.

Cauliflower has a winter reputation, and it will indeed carry as many of the cold weather preparations as you might need. But it is also a gentle youth in early summer, when the heads are much smaller and the cooking time shorter. Blanch a very fresh head of cauliflower for only two minutes, break it into florets with a fork, and sauté the pieces with early summer garlic and greens, and you will discover what a sweet cabbage it is.

Cauliflower with Sage and Peperoncini

1 medium head cauliflower

¼ cup (60 ml) extra-virgin olive oil, plus more for drizzling

1 fresh peperoncino (see Note), sliced crosswise into rings

Sea salt

6 to 8 fresh sage leaves

¼ cup (25 g) freshly grated Parmigiano-Reggiano cheese

Fresh cracked black pepper

SERVES 4

Once you start treating cauliflower like it is fun, all sorts of things become possible. In this dish, the cauliflower is browned and stirred with the sage leaves and the small red Tuscan peppers known as peperoncini fresh (the ripened version of the green peppers you often find in jars): It is a dish that comes together quickly and has the lovely juxtaposition of the green sage, the bright red peperoncino, and the pale white cauliflower. It is an elegant—and surprising—hors d'oeuvre, and a lovely side dish.

Trim the cauliflower and set it in a large bowl of cold water to soak for 10 minutes. Drain it well.

Bring a big pot of water to a boil. Cut an X in the stem end of the cauliflower and put it into the boiling water, X side down. Cook for 6 minutes, then check the progress by poking the florets with a fork to test for softening. It may need to cook for up to 6 minutes more. When the cauliflower is soft but not mushy, drain it well.

In a large sauté pan, heat the olive oil over medium heat. Break the cauliflower head into florets and cut the stem into bite-size pieces. Add the peperoncino to the pan and, seconds later, the cauliflower, and give the pan a shake to mix and coat with the olive oil. Salt the cauliflower— it will need it.

Throw the sage leaves into the mix, toss and toss, browning the cauliflower, and 2 minutes later it should be ready. Turn the heat off, add a little of the cheese so it can melt a bit, and lay the cauliflower on a warmed plate.

Add some cracked black pepper, more salt, and the remaining cheese. Finish with a good line of olive oil.

NOTE: Taste a small piece of the peperoncino. It should only be medium-hot. If it's very hot, only use half.

Cauliflower Baked in Butter and Parmesan

1 medium head cauliflower

Sea salt

4 tablespoons (½ stick/55 g) cold, unsalted butter

½ cup (50 g) freshly grated Parmigiano-Reggiano cheese, plus more for finishing

SERVES 4

This dish will help convert anyone who has steered clear of cauliflower. The melted butter, Parmesan cheese, and salt are somewhat unfair to any sample, but it is still the cauliflower that makes the dish work. Serve it with any kind of seared meat or alongside a vegetable sauté.

Preheat the oven to 400°F (205°C).

Trim the cauliflower and set it in a large bowl of cold water to soak for 10 minutes. Drain it well.

Bring a big pot of water to a boil. Cut an X in the stem end of the cauliflower and put it into the boiling water, X side down. Cook for 6 minutes, then check the progress by poking the florets with a fork to test for softening. It may need to cook for up to 6 minutes more. When the cauliflower is soft but not mushy, drain it well and let cool a bit. Break the cauliflower head into florets and cut the stem into bite-size pieces; season the lot with salt.

Set a baking dish in the oven for a minute or two to warm. Add 1 table-spoon of the butter to the warmed dish so it melts; tilt the dish so the butter coats the bottom. Sprinkle a pinch of the cheese over the butter and then arrange the cauliflower florets in the dish.

Sprinkle it all well with the remaining cheese and season with a little salt. Cut the remaining 3 tablespoons butter into cubes and dot them over the cauliflower. Roast for 20 minutes, until the cauliflower has browned a little and parts of the grated cheese have hardened.

Sprinkle with even a little more cheese after it comes out of the oven—and perhaps some salt. The salt keeps it all in line.

Cauliflower with Penne Pasta and Pancetta Bread Crumbs

1 medium head cauliflower

2 prunes, chopped

1 tablespoon dry Marsala

4 tablespoons (½ stick/55 g) cold, unsalted butter

¼ pound (115 g) pancetta, sliced into skinny strips

1½ cups (150 g) crisp bread crumbs

Pinch of red pepper flakes

Sea salt and fresh ground black pepper

½ pound (225 g) good-quality dried penne pasta

¼ cup (60 ml) extra-virgin olive oil, plus more for drizzling

¼ cup (25 g) freshly grated Parmigiano-Reggiano cheese

SERVES 4

I made this dish for many years before I made it correctly. It needed something—a detail. There is a recipe in the book *Canal House Cooks Every Day* that fixed it. Here is my version of it, with all credit to *les Canalistes*. It is just the thing, this bread crumb topping, with its salty bits of pork, the sweet prune, the crisp bread crumbs, a little spice, and a little pepper.

Trim the cauliflower and set it in a large bowl of cold water to soak for 10 minutes. In a separate small bowl, soak the prunes in the Marsala. Drain both well.

Heat a sauté pan over medium heat. Add 2 tablespoons of the butter and the pancetta. Let it brown, stirring often. Add the bread crumbs, stir to combine, and let them brown as well, about 10 minutes. Turn off the heat and add the red pepper flakes, prunes and Marsala, salt, and a couple grinds of black pepper.

Bring a big pot of water to a boil. Cut an X in the stem end of the cauliflower and put it into the boiling water, X side down. Cook for 6 minutes, then check the progress by poking the florets with a fork to test for softening. It may need to cook for up to 6 minutes more. When the cauliflower is soft but not mushy, drain it well and let cool a bit. Break the cauliflower head into florets and cut the stem into bite-size pieces; season the lot with salt.

Heat another sauté pan over medium-high heat. Add the olive oil and the cauliflower. You want to brown the cauliflower and you will need some heat to do it. You will need to keep tossing it about in the pan. Add some salt and black pepper and keep it all very sprightly. You will see and smell the cauliflower browning and caramelizing. Turn the heat down a bit and add the drained pasta and some salt.

Quickly stir together the cauliflower and the pasta. Taste and adjust the seasoning, then add the remaining 2 tablespoons butter and 1 or 2 tablespoons of the reserved pasta water to make a light sauce. Serve in warmed pasta bowls, topped with the cheese, a generous handful of the bread crumbs, and one last grind of pepper. You might add a line of olive oil as well.

Pan-Roasted Cauliflower with a Salad

1 tablespoon white wine vinegar

2 tablespoons fresh lemon juice

Sea salt

½ teaspoon Colman's dry
mustard

1 garlic clove, crushed

½ cup (120 ml) extra-virgin
olive oil

1 small head cauliflower

¼ cup (60 ml) extra-virgin
olive oil

Fresh ground black pepper

2 tablespoons cold, unsalted
butter

1 garlic clove, thinly sliced

2 tablespoons chicken stock,
at a simmer

2 tablespoons chopped fresh
flat-leaf parsley

1 pound (455 g) mixed salad
greens, the wilder the better,
rinsed and spun dry

Small bunch of chives

¼ cup (25 g) freshly grated
Parmigiano-Reggiano cheese

SERVES 4

This preparation of cauliflower can be a simple side dish. The cauliflower can also join easily with some greens. Make the vinaigrette twenty minutes before serving, so it can settle.

Trim the cauliflower and set it in a large bowl of cold water to soak for 10 minutes. Drain it well.

Bring a big pot of water to a boil. Cut an X in the stem end of the cauliflower and put it into the boiling water, X side down. Cook for 6 minutes, then check the progress by poking the florets with a fork to test for softening. It may need to cook for up to 6 minutes more. When the cauliflower is soft but not mushy, drain it well and let cool a bit. Break the cauliflower head into florets then into smaller pieces, and season them with salt.

In a 10-inch (25-cm) sauté pan, heat the olive oil over medium heat. Add the cauliflower—it should sizzle a bit. Shake the pan to coat the cauliflower with the oil and add a grind of black pepper.

When the cauliflower begins to brown, turn the heat down just a bit and add the butter and the garlic. Stir it all well, add the stock, and stir again. You should smell the garlic and the cauliflower. Add the parsley, stir, and turn off the heat.

In a small bowl, use a fork to mix the vinegar, lemon juice, and some salt. Let sit for a minute to dissolve. Add the mustard and garlic, stir with the fork to combine, then slowly stir in the olive oil. The dressing should thicken as you mix. Add a few drops of cold water to thicken it further.

Put the greens in a large salad bowl. Add the dressing and toss well. Grind some pepper over the top. Toss the chives about like pick-up sticks, then lay the roasted cauliflower across the top. Finish with the cheese and more pepper and salt.

Cauliflower and Corn Duet

1 pound (455 g) cauliflower

2 or 3 fresh ears of corn, shucked

Sea salt and fresh ground black pepper

½ pound (225 g) wild mushrooms (optional)

2 tablespoon extra-virgin olive oil, plus a little to finish

2 tablespoon cold, unsalted butter

1 garlic clove, minced

Pinch of red pepper flakes

¼ cup (25 g) freshly grated Parmigiano-Reggiano cheese

6 to 8 fresh basil leaves, torn into smaller pieces

SERVES 4

This is a wonderful addition to a barbecue. It can be cooked right over the fire. I did not think of pairing corn and cauliflower until someone held three ears of corn up that had been cooked but forgotten, right at the moment that I was about to quickly sauté some cauliflower in olive oil and garlic over a wood fire. Now it seems a natural pairing to me, of sweet taste and texture.

Bring a large pot of water to a boil.

Trim the cauliflower and set it in a large bowl of cold water to soak for 10 minutes. Drain well and cut the cauliflower into florets and its stem into smaller pieces.

Toss the corn into the boiling water. Cook for 3 minutes, then remove with tongs and set in a colander to drain and cool. Add the cauliflower florets and stems to the boiling water and cook until softened, 3 to 5 minutes, depending on freshness. It is better they be slightly underdone than soft and mushy. Drain the cauliflower and salt it. (Never start with the cauliflower. It leaves too strong a taste in the water.)

Stand the corn on one end in a bowl and slice the kernels downward into the bowl. Add some salt and pepper.

Heat a 10-inch (25-cm) sauté pan over medium heat for 30 seconds. Add the olive oil and butter. When the butter foams, add the garlic, red pepper flakes, cauliflower, and mushrooms (if using) and cook, shaking the pan and stirring to mix them, for 3 minutes. Do not let the garlic brown.

Add the corn kernels to the pan and mix them well with some good shakes of the pan. The corn need only cook for a minute or so. Toss in half the cheese and a few grinds of black pepper, give the pan one more shake, and turn it out into a warmed shallow serving bowl. Top with the rest of the cheese, the basil, a bit of salt, and a drizzle of olive oil.

THE BASE OF YOUR MEAL

Legumes, Rice, Pasta, and More

Beans, lentils, rice, pasta, quinoa, and couscous are a
welcoming foundation for a vast range of meals. But to work
well, the meals must also have a grace and an allure; they
must have a depth and a subtlety. Trust the basic elements—
they do not need great fanfare to make their entrance.
They simply need your attention.

No one talked about beans, lentils, quinoa, and such when
I was growing up—there was no language or detail for them.
But now, they are coming out of the dullness of a Cold War.
Instead of simply "red beans" or "black or white beans,"
they are recovering their actual names—cannellini, alubia,
cranberry (Borlotti), scarlet runner, ayocote, flageolet.
The names of lentils are like a travel brochure—lenticchie,
beluga, puy, masoor.

As you make distinctions among your ingredients, you grow
closer to what you are cooking, and you become more
aware of the process. That intimacy is reflected in your food.

FIVE WAYS TO COOK
Beans

If you make a habit of cooking dried beans, the task will quickly become as automatic as cleaning the counters. Cannellini beans, cranberry beans, great Northerns, kidney beans—they are all perfect allies. Once you have beans that are cooked, then you have the options of things you can do with them.

Beans have carried many meals for hundreds of years. You will learn to trust them and even to lean on them. I have detailed five of my favorite dishes that rely on cooked beans—they are a good place to start. If you are looking for a tried and true method for cooking them, see page 234.

Be certain that the beans you are buying are no more than a year or so old. It is difficult to judge their age by appearance—you must trust their source. We have been buying our beans from Rancho Gordo, either directly or in some of the food shops that stock their products. Beans that have been dried within the year cook more quickly and are distinctly creamier—a fine quality when you are making a cannellini bean soup, for example.

Cannellini Beans with Cured Ham, Sage, and Arugula

4 tablespoons (60 ml) extra-
  virgin olive oil

¼ pound (115 g) prosciutto
  or serrano ham, thinly sliced
  into strips

2 garlic cloves, crushed

2 cups (310 g) cooked cannellini
  beans, drained, at room
  temperature (page 234)

Sea salt and fresh ground black
  pepper

1 tablespoon red wine vinegar

2 cups (40 g) arugula, washed
  and dried

6 fresh sage leaves

SERVES 4

You can put this out before a meal or with a meal. It is the pleasure of beans. I like to serve it with toast or bruschetta to the side. The task is the work and attention to have the beans ready—soaking, rinsing, cooking slowly, and so forth. I always store the cooked beans in a clear glass container in the fridge. When I get home and there is a meal to make, I can see the beans and I know they are ready to work.

Heat a sauté pan over medium heat. Add 1 tablespoon of the olive oil, the prosciutto, and the garlic and cook, stirring a few times, until the prosciutto begins to brown and separate. Add the beans, some salt and pepper, and sauté for a minute more, to warm the beans and mix. Turn off the heat and add the vinegar.

Put the arugula in a bowl, add some salt, and mix for a moment. Pour the beans and prosciutto over the greens. Stir them gently, then add the remaining 3 tablespoons olive oil.

Lay it out in a shallow serving bowl, season with salt and pepper, and arrange the sage leaves on top.

Bean Salad with Tuna and Red Onions

1 medium red onion, thinly sliced
and rinsed

Sea salt

½ lemon

1 small fresh red chile, seeded
and finely chopped (see Note)

¼ cup (60 ml) extra-virgin
olive oil

Fresh ground black pepper

1 cup (155 g) cooked cannellini
beans, drained (page 234)

1 (7-ounce/200-g) can tuna
packed in olive oil, drained

1 tablespoon red wine vinegar

SERVES 4

**I do not like bean salad, as a takeout meal or as a phrase, and use
it here in hopes of upending its dull tyranny and rebranding it as a
bright-eyed star.**

**Find a good can of Italian or Portuguese tuna for this dish—or find
the season for tuna caught nearest to you and poach your own.
And make certain the beans have come to room temperature, or
their taste will be muted.**

**Serve this salad modestly, so the parts are all obvious. It would be
wonderful as a lunch, and perfect to follow a light pasta dish at dinner.**

Soak the onion slices in a bowl of cold water with a pinch of salt for at
least 30 minutes. Drain and rinse them, then dry them well with paper
towels so they have a slight crunch to them.

Return them to the bowl and add the lemon juice, chile, a little of the
olive oil, salt, and black pepper.

Put the cannellini beans in a serving bowl, add the onions and all their
dressing, and toss once or twice. Add the tuna, breaking it up with a
fork. Add the rest of the olive oil, the vinegar, and several grindings of
black pepper. Taste and adjust the seasoning, then serve.

NOTE: If the chile is very hot, use only half.

Cannellini Beans with Pancetta, Red Potatoes, and Spinach

Sea salt

½ pound (225 g) small red
potatoes

I pound (455 g) spinach,
stemmed

¼ cup (60 ml) extra-virgin
olive oil

¼ pound (115 g) pancetta, cut
into thin strips

2 garlic cloves, minced

Fresh ground black pepper

I cup (155 g) cooked cannellini
beans or cranberry beans,
drained, at room temperature
(page 234)

I tablespoon red wine vinegar

SERVES 4

There are times when this dish is a meal to itself—especially if you have fresh country white bread to eat and dip with it. And there are times that it would make an elegant first course. It is a good-looking group—the lovely white beans, the red potatoes in halves, the deep green spinach, and the bits of pancetta. I want them to be visible and not appear bulky at all. There is some fussing with the construction, keeping the elements separate before they join up. Move quickly and you will hardly notice.

Bring a medium saucepan of water to a boil. Add a good pinch of salt and the potatoes and cook until they just begin to soften, about 15 minutes. Drain and let cool, then cut them in half.

Heat a large sauté pan over medium heat. Quickly rinse a handful of the spinach in the sink and add it to the pan, stirring, then rinse and add the rest. The spinach will begin to wilt immediately. Add some salt and cover the pan. Cook for 3 to 5 minutes, depending on the freshness of the spinach. It will reduce in volume very quickly. Stir and do not let it dry out. You may need to add a tablespoon of water if that is the case—you are simply cooking the leaves in moisture, until they soften.

Drain the spinach quickly, using a rubber spatula to push out extra moisture. Then put the spinach on the cutting board, salt it a little, and coarsely chop it.

Heat two sauté pans over medium heat. To one pan, add a little olive oil and all the pancetta and let it brown for 3 to 4 minutes. To the other, add the rest of the olive oil and the garlic and, a few moments later, the chopped spinach. Stir well, add some pepper, and make certain the garlic does not brown but instead gets caught up in the spinach. Add the potatoes and mix well. Turn off the heat.

When the pancetta has browned, add the cannellini beans to the pan and toss to combine. Add the potatoes and the spinach and stir lightly to combine.

Add the vinegar, more pepper, and some salt, and the dish is ready. The vinegar will make it all more distinct. When you serve it, use a warmed wide soup bowl and add extra olive oil and cracked pepper to the outer edges of the bowl, for color and taste.

White Bean Soup and the Chanterelles

2 cups (480 ml) homemade chicken stock (page 35)

¼ cup (60 ml) extra-virgin olive oil

3 garlic cloves, 2 minced, 1 thinly sliced

1½ cups (230 g) cooked cannellini beans, at room temperature (page 234)

Sea salt

¼ cup (13 g) chopped fresh flat-leaf parsley

3 tablespoons cold, unsalted butter

½ pound (225 g) fresh chanterelles, quartered

Fresh ground black pepper

1 teaspoon grated lemon zest

SERVES 4

Making a cannellini bean soup in the spring, with the first of the garlic and the parsley, seems quite natural. But making the same soup in the fall, with the fresh wild mushrooms, is a treat. The mushrooms are the color and the taste of fall, and the creamy white bean soup loves the company.

If you have some good country white bread, cut a slice for each bowl. Brown it in olive oil and poke it into the soup.

In a small pot, bring the stock to a simmer.

In a heavy pan, heat half the olive oil over medium heat. After a few moments, add the minced garlic, then the beans. Stir to incorporate and add a good pinch of salt. Turn down the heat a little and cover the pan for a couple of minutes to build the flavors.

Scoop half the beans into a food mill and pass them back into the pan. (Alternatively, pulse them in a food processor until pureed, then return them to the pan.) Slowly add two-thirds of the simmering stock. The mash and the stock will merge and combine to a creamy texture. Taste and adjust the seasoning, and be careful to stir. Add half the parsley and 1 tablespoon of the butter and turn the heat to very low. If the soup should start to stick, add a little more stock.

While the soup cooks, in a 10-inch (25-cm) sauté pan, heat the rest of the olive oil and the remaining 2 tablespoons butter over medium heat. Quickly add the mushrooms, sliced garlic, and some salt and pepper, and stir to incorporate. Toss the mixture a couple of times and let the edges of the mushrooms slightly sear, a minute or two. Then add half a ladle of the stock—it will bubble and pull up anything stuck to the sur-face of the pan. As the stock cooks off, taste the mushrooms. If they are still too firm, add a little more stock and test again. Season the mush-rooms with salt and pepper and pull them out of the pan with a slotted spoon. Lay them on a warm plate. Use your judgment with the sauce in the pan—if it needs a little more liquid to even out, add it and stir to combine. If it is too loose, let the heat thicken it. You want a gravy that will touch both the mushrooms and the soup below, binding them.

Ladle the creamy soup into warmed bowls. Lay the mushrooms on top, covering about half the surface of the soup. Then carefully spoon a trail of the sauce across the mushrooms, touching the soup on each side. Finish each serving with a pinch of the lemon zest, some of the remain-ing parsley, and some pepper.

Cranberry Bean and Rice Soup
with Swiss Chard

3 cups (530 g) cooked cranberry
(Borlotti) beans, stored in
their cooking liquid (page 234)

¼ cup (60 ml) extra-virgin olive
oil, plus more as needed

1 medium red or yellow onion,
finely chopped

1 carrot, finely chopped

1 celery stalk, finely chopped

2 or 3 fresh sage leaves, chopped

Sea salt and fresh ground black
pepper

½ cup (95 g) Arborio rice

2 tablespoons cold, unsalted
butter

½ pound (225 g) Swiss chard,
leaves and stems chopped into
2-inch (5-cm) pieces

¼ cup (13 g) chopped fresh flat-
leaf parsley

6 slices of good country bread

1 garlic clove

SERVES 4

If you made this soup every week, it would seem quite straightforward. It is a wonderfully simple meal, but at first, it looks like a task. Once you get a sense of it, a habit of it, then it is easily done. It makes a fine dinner and an envied lunch. But there are a few details to the preparation, and they stretch over a couple of days. You can also add the roasted cauliflower (page 130) for added detail and texture.

Drain the beans and carefully save the liquid they were soaking in. If there is time, let the beans come to room temperature.

In a small saucepan, heat 1 cup (240 ml) water over low heat. (I try to do this whenever I am making a soup or sauce—and if on my toes, I add bits of garlic, onion, parsley stems, or the end of a carrot to the pan as they come available and clog up the corners of the cutting board. You could of course use a beef, chicken, or vegetable stock.)

Heat a good ceramic or stainless-steel pot over medium heat for a couple of minutes. Add half the olive oil, the onion, carrot, celery, and sage. Cook for 5 minutes to soften the vegetables, then season with salt and pepper. Add the drained beans, reserving ½ cup (90 g) to add later, and stir well to combine. Cook the bean and vegetable mixture for 10 minutes, stirring frequently. You can add a little more olive oil if they stick to the pan too much; you can also turn the heat down a little.

Transfer the contents of the pot to a food processor and process until smooth. Return the puree to the pot, add some salt, pepper, and 2 cups (480 ml) of the bean soaking liquid, and bring the mixture to a slow boil. You must stir carefully—the smooth beans will be like a paste until they absorb the liquid, and you do not want anything to burn. Add the reserved beans. Add ¼ to ½ cup (60 to 120 ml)—or more—hot water to the soup. You want a smooth, gravylike consistency, which gathers all the liquids together. But it must be thin enough to still cook the rice.

Add the rice to the softly boiling soup, with a slight drizzle of the olive oil on top, and stir to incorporate. Cook for 15 minutes, making certain the soup is loose enough to not clog up during the cooking time.

While the rice is cooking, heat a sauté pan over medium heat. Add a little olive oil and 1 tablespoon of the butter to it, and when it foams, add the chard, a little salt and pepper, and a pinch of the parsley. Stir well to coat the chard. Turn down the heat slightly, cover, and cook at a lively but not wild pace for 4 minutes or so. If they seem a little dry, add a tablespoon of your hot water. When they have absorbed most of the liquid but are still a little firm, turn off the heat and set aside.

When the rice is cooked, stir the chard and the remaining 1 tablespoon butter into the soup.

Grill or broil the bread quickly. When browned, rub it immediately with the garlic. Drizzle some olive oil over each piece and then sprinkle with some salt, pepper, and a little parsley. With a sharp knife, cut the bread into strips or triangles.

Ladle the soup into warmed soup bowls, being careful to stir it well first. To each, add a couple of pieces of the grilled bread on top, a tiny line of olive oil, whatever parsley is left, a little pepper, and even the bread crumbs from the cutting board. Soup is ready.

FIVE WAYS TO COOK

Rice

Learn your rice. I cook with carnaroli and Arborio rice, with Spanish bomba and basmati rice, and each is particularly apt for certain dishes. But they are only a sample—there are many other types of rice.

The supermarkets have made rice a dullard and made it a pretension to look for anything more than a long-grain white. But you are not still shaking your Parmesan from a green can, and you should not settle for a sullen, nameless rice. (It did turn out that the Parmesan cheese in the green cardboard tube was not cheese at all, let alone Parmesan.)

Once you have ventured into the varieties of rice, then you can experiment with how you want to cook them. I began making risotto with Arborio rice, a stubby grain that seemed perfect to me. But then someone gave me some carnaroli rice, a slimmer, longer grain, and it made the simplest risottos—the Milanese, for example—even more elegant, for it produced a silkier finish.

When I am cooking rice for itself, I will always use the best basmati brand I can find. There have been many scandals that involve basmati. It is itself a rather pure strain of rice. Like the true Parmigiano-Reggiano, there are many imitators that have used the name *basmati* to sell much lesser strains of the rice. Look carefully at the package. It should confirm at least some authenticity, referencing *Basmati*, as opposed to *Basmati-like*. Basmati is most famous for its aroma, a wonderful smell that justifies its elegance.

Store your rice in clear, airtight glass containers. Many things, some on foot and some by wing, would love to get into the lovely grains.

Here are five of my best recipes for rice, using several varieties and a few techniques to give a sense of the simple brilliance of rice.

Rice with Egg, Pancetta, and Parmesan

3 cups (720 ml) homemade
chicken stock (page 35)

¼ cup (60 ml) extra-virgin
olive oil

2 tablespoons unsalted butter

¼ pound (115 g) pancetta, thinly
sliced into small strips

2 tablespoons finely chopped
onion

1 tablespoon finely chopped
garlic

1 cup (190 g) carnaroli rice

¼ cup (60 ml) dry white wine

Sea salt

4 fresh organic eggs, medium
or large size, at room
temperature

1 tablespoon white wine vinegar

½ cup (50 g) freshly grated
Parmigiano-Reggiano

½ cup (25 g) chopped fresh
flat-leaf parsley

Fresh ground black pepper

SERVES 4

This is a hat tipped to pasta carbonara. It is easily prepared if you are careful to have Italian rice and pancetta on hand. The stubby carnaroli is important because the grain soaks up the liquid and softens to a plump size. Do not use bacon; it would be too sweet and throw off the balance of the dish.

In a small pot, bring the stock to a simmer.

Heat a heavy-bottomed pan, with a good lid, over medium heat. Add the olive oil and butter. When the butter has melted, add the pancetta, onion, and garlic. Cook for 8 to 10 minutes, stirring often, until the pancetta darkens and the onion turns yellow. Add the rice and cook, stirring, for 2 minutes, then add the wine. When the wine has evaporated, 2 minutes or so, add some salt and enough stock to cover the rice by 1 inch (2.5 cm). Bring the stock to a boil, then turn the temperature down a bit to maintain a simmer and cover the pan. Simmer for 15 minutes or so, until the rice is al dente (slightly firm)—test with a wooden spoon that there is no more liquid at the very bottom and the rice is softened.

Meanwhile, bring a medium saucepan of water to a boil, then reduce the heat to maintain a simmer. Break the eggs into a cup, being careful that they remain whole. Add the vinegar to the simmering water and gently slide the eggs into the pan. Turn off the heat. Cover the pan, and in 4 minutes, lift out the softly poached eggs with a slotted spoon.

When the rice is ready, turn off the heat, sprinkle some of the cheese over the surface, and put the lid back on. Let rest for 2 minutes.

Stir the rice well to lighten it, and serve it in warmed bowls. Lay the poached eggs on the rice, half broken so the yolks can seep a little. Finish with more cheese, the parsley, and some pepper. Serve immediately—it is important that the rice and the egg still be quite hot.

Rice in an Ode to Fall

4 to 6 cups (960 ml to 1.2 L)
homemade chicken or
vegetable stock (pages 35–36)

¼ cup (60 ml) extra-virgin
olive oil

4 tablespoons (½ stick/55 g)
very cold, unsalted butter

1 medium red onion, chopped as
finely as rice

1 medium late-season carrot,
shaved and cut into sticks

1 red bell pepper, cut into strips

8 to 10 green beans, trimmed
and carefully halved lengthwise

1 cup (190 g) Arborio rice

¼ cup (60 ml) dry white wine

1 cup (145 g) fresh peas

Sea salt

1 or 2 ripe, fresh tomatoes,
peeled, seeded, and diced

½ cup (20 g) chopped fresh basil

1 roasted chicken breast (see
page 209), plus any extra meat,
cut into bite-size pieces

½ pound (225 g) chanterelle
mushrooms, cleaned and cut
into 2-inch (5-cm) pieces

Fresh ground black pepper

½ cup (25 g) chopped fresh flat-
leaf parsley

1 cup (100 g) freshly grated
Parmigiano-Reggiano
cheese or a combination of
Parmigiano-Reggiano and
Pecorino Romano

SERVES 4

This risotto is a nod to summer's end and to fall's dignity, and it has
become a great favorite. In the Pacific Northwest, the vegetables and
herbs are all at the end of their season by September. They harden
a little. But cooked in the heat of a risotto and broth, they seem to
sparkle, especially the peas and green beans and that last local carrot.
You can make this recipe at any time, of course, but it does have a
special taste when it comes at the end of the season.

When I serve it, I want the mushrooms stacked carelessly atop the
risotto, a jumble of them, like the garden tools after the first frost.
This is a risotto for the first fall night that you need a sweater and
warmer socks.

I typically make this recipe after roasting a chicken the day before. It
is, in a way, a meal of leftovers—vegetables from the summer, a little
chicken, the slight tomato taste and color, the wonderful green peas
scattered around, and then the fresh, wild chanterelles sitting up top.

In a small pot, bring the stock to a simmer.

In a large, heavy stainless-steel or ceramic pot, heat half the olive oil and
half the butter over medium to medium-high heat—hot enough to be
lively, but not enough to scorch and burn. When the butter is foaming,
add the onion, reserving 1 tablespoon to cook with the mushrooms.
Cook, stirring, for 2 minutes, until the onion has softened. Add the
carrot, bell pepper, and green beans and stir. Cook for 4 minutes. Using
tongs, carefully lift out some of the peppers, carrots, and green beans
and set them aside in a bowl (they are going back into the risotto in 15
minutes or so—you are taking them out so they will retain some texture).

Add the rice, stir well, and let it toast, stirring, for 2 minutes. You should
be able to smell its nutty flavor. Add the wine. It will sizzle and cook away
in a minute or two. Begin adding ladles of the hot stock, one at a time.
The stock should cover the rice but not drown it. You will be busy; this
is no time for phone calls. Add the peas and a sprinkle of salt and stir.

Continue to add stock, one or two ladles at a time, and stir near continuously for about 18 minutes, while the risotto gets slightly heavier as it
absorbs the liquid and expands. Be careful to stir deeply and not let any
surface burn or get too dry. Each moment that the rice begins to dry out
and stick, add more stock. After 10 minutes, stir in the tomatoes and half

the basil. After 15 minutes, the rice should have expanded and become heavy with the moisture of the stock. Add back the vegetables and fold in the chicken. For the last 2 or 3 minutes, you can use less stock, but you must stir more and be more vigilant that the rice not stick to the bottom of the pan. You have added bulk to the rice, so bend your knees and stir deep into the pan. Taste the rice at 18 minutes—it should be tender but still have the slightest bite. If not—if it is too firm—cook for another minute or so, stirring and adding a little more stock. You may not use all the stock—that is fine.

While the risotto is cooking, heat a sauté pan over medium heat. Add 1 tablespoon each of the remaining olive oil and butter and the reserved 1 tablespoon onion. Shake the pan to mix them and cook for 1 minute. Add the chanterelles and shake the pan again to mix. Cook for a minute, then turn the heat down a little and throw in a pinch of salt, black pepper, and a little parsley. If the pan seems dry, add a tablespoon or two of the stock. If there is too much liquid, turn up the heat slightly. Cook, shaking the pan every 30 seconds or so, until the mushrooms are softened but not limp and only a little moisture remains. Remove from the heat and set aside.

Remove the risotto pan from the heat, cover, and let it rest for 1 minute. Stir the remaining 1 tablespoon butter into the risotto, with hefty turns to get it deep into the rice and to have it melt evenly. Stir for 1 minute, then add half the cheese and stir to coat the rice. If the risotto seems too thick, add a tablespoon or two of the stock. Taste and adjust the seasoning. It will likely need some salt and black pepper.

Moving quickly to protect the temperature, spoon the risotto into warmed bowls. Top with a little of the Parmesan, the remaining basil, a nice spoonful of the chanterelles laid gently on the surface, the remaining parsley, a tiny bit more salt and black pepper, and a thin drizzle of olive oil. There should be a little grated cheese left to put on the table.

Rice and Its Many Partners

2 tablespoons plain Greek yogurt

Salt

Extra-virgin olive oil

2 tablespoons cooked white
    beans (optional)

Fresh ground black pepper

2 tablespoons chopped fresh
    flat-leaf parsley

2 tablespoons chopped fresh
    cilantro

Heaping serving spoon of cooked
    basmati rice, warm, salted, and
    peppered (see page 235)

2 tablespoons mango chutney

2 tablespoons hummus

2 tablespoons plum sauce

2 tablespoons hot sauce

1 tablespoon pesto

1 tablespoon black olive
    tapenade

2 tablespoons sesame seeds

6 to 8 pita breads (see page 54)

Flaky sea salt

SERVES 4, AS A STARTER OR SNACK

The rice can be cooked in practically any fashion. Typically, I will use basmati rice, for its aroma.

This is a way of appreciating how rice loves to partner with many flavors. The rice is set out with a plate of warm pita and two plates of sauces and herbs. It is an assembly of varying tastes—there is no right or wrong. The rice is the ambassador of all the elements, making each one feel at home. You should think of it as a medley, of taste and color. You can use any of the condiments in your pantry; this is a chance to bring them out. The rice makes it all possible.

To the yogurt, add a pinch of salt and stir in a thin line of olive oil, leaving a little of the oil to be seen on top. If using the white beans, mix them first in a small bowl, adding a good pinch of salt and then some olive oil. Crack pepper on top of the yogurt and beans.

Lay the herbs, rice, and sauces around a platter of rice to create a palette of ingredients.

Heat a cast-iron pan over low heat for 5 minutes or in a preheated 300°F (150°C) oven for the same time. Once hot, put the sesame seeds in the pan for a couple of minutes, to freshen and slightly toast them, and then pour the sesame seeds loosely over some of the condiments.

Heat a little olive oil in the pan and add a couple pieces of pita to warm and brown slightly.

When they are warmed but still supple, stack the pitas and cut them into thirds. Lay them on the platter with the rice. Sprinkle some olive oil across them and some good flaky salt. The meal, as such, is ready.

The sauces can be used individually or mixed with herbs and the yogurt. Typically, I will choose one of the sauces, lay that on the piece of pita, add some rice, then perhaps yogurt and a pinch of the chopped herbs.

Rice and Luganega Sausage Soup

5 to 6 cups (1.2 to 1.4 L)
homemade chicken stock
(page 35)

2 tablespoons extra-virgin olive
oil, plus more as needed

2 tablespoons cold, unsalted
butter

1 small yellow onion or shallot,
chopped as fine as rice

½ pound (225 g) luganega
sausage, casings removed

1 cup (190 g) Arborio rice

½ cup (120 ml) dry white wine

½ pound (225 g) Swiss chard,
leaves and stems chopped and
kept separate

Sea salt and fresh cracked black
pepper

½ cup (50 g) freshly grated
Parmigiano-Reggiano cheese

¼ cup (13 g) finely chopped
fresh flat-leaf parsley

SERVES 4

**This is probably a winter soup, but really you just need the weather
to be unfavorable and the sausage to be fresh. It has elements of
a risotto, but more elements of a good hearty soup. The luganega
sausage is typically sold in a coil, not in links, and is always fresh.
While any sausage could work, it has more of a taste of herbs than of
spice, making it a good partner for soup.**

In a small pot, bring the stock to a simmer.

Heat a heavy saucepan over medium heat. Add the olive oil and the
butter and, a minute later, the onion. When the onion begins to color,
add the sausage. Cook, stirring and breaking it up with a wooden spoon
as it browns, for 6 to 8 minutes.

Add the rice and cook, stirring, for 2 minutes to slightly toast the
grains. Then, add the wine, stir, and let it cook away completely.

Add about three-quarters of the stock, stir, and bring it to a low simmer. Simmer, stirring often, for 18 to 20 minutes, until the rice is tender
but still has a slight bite. When the rice is done, check the soup. If it
seems too thick, add some or all of the reserved stock.

In the meantime, in a small sauté pan, heat a little olive oil over medium
heat. Add the chard stems and a bit of salt and pepper, and sauté for 4
minutes, until soft. Add the chard leaves, stir to combine, and remove
from the heat. When the soup is nearly done, add the chard to it.

Turn off the heat under the soup. Add half the cheese and half the
parsley. Stir to combine. Let the soup set for a minute or two. Taste and
adjust the seasoning.

Serve in warmed bowls, with more of the cheese and parsley scattered
on top. Finish with cracked pepper and a little olive oil.

Rice in the Oven with Tomatoes, Peas, and Mozzarella

4 cups (960 ml) homemade
chicken stock (page 35)

7 tablespoons (90 ml) extra-
virgin olive oil, plus extra
as needed

1 medium onion, finely chopped

2 garlic cloves, crushed a little

1½ cups (300 g) carnaroli or
Spanish Valencia rice

Sea salt

¼ cup (60 ml) dry white wine

½ cup (70 g) defrosted frozen or
fresh peas, rinsed

½ pound (225 g) fresh
mozzarella, cut into ¼-inch
(6-mm) slices

12 cherry tomatoes

2 tablespoons cold, unsalted
butter

½ cup (50 g) freshly grated
Parmigiano-Reggiano cheese

12 to 16 fresh basil leaves,
torn a little

Fresh ground black pepper

SERVES 4

**You begin as if you were starting a risotto, and you end, in much the
same way, stirring in cold butter and adding grated cheese. At the
start, you can add items that would be bulky for a risotto. And at the
finish, you can use the steam to cook softer vegetables, mushrooms,
and fruits. Lay them quickly on the surface when the pan comes out
and leave the heavy lid on to do the steaming.**

In a small pot, bring the stock to a simmer.

Preheat the oven to 400°F (205°C).

Heat a heavy ovenproof pan with a lid over medium heat. Add 4 tablespoons (60 ml) of the olive oil, then add the onion and garlic and stir
well. Cook for 6 to 8 minutes, until the onion softens, then add the rice
and a good pinch of salt, and stir well to combine. Toast the rice for 2
to 3 minutes, but do not let it burn. Add the wine; it will cook off in a
minute or so. Stir the rice once, then add enough stock to cover the
rice by 1 inch (2.5 cm); you may not need to use all the stock. Put 1
more tablespoon of oil on the top, cover, and get the pan into the oven.

Bake the rice for 25 minutes. Carefully lift it out of the oven. Have your
additional ingredients ready—you do not want to lose the heat and
steam. Quickly, lift the lid and sprinkle on the peas, mozzarella, tomatoes,
and a good pinch of salt. Cover the pan and set it aside for 5 minutes.

Uncover the pan to add the butter. Stir well for a minute and add most
of the cheese. Stir once or twice to incorporate. Taste and add some
of the basil, some salt and pepper, and the remaining 2 tablespoons
olive oil. Serve immediately with the rest of the basil and more cheese
scattered over the top.

VARIATIONS: You could easily add 4 to 6 asparagus spears to the rice.
Peel the asparagus and blanch for 3 minutes. Cut the tips from the stems
and set them aside. Cut the stems into 2-inch (5-cm) pieces and add them
just before the rice is added. Save the tips and add them when you put
the cherry tomatoes in. The slight steaming will bring out their best!

FIVE WAYS TO COOK
Lentils

They are a quiet royalty, lentils. I have only begun to learn how to use them well. Lentils, after all, are not the first legume to be considered—if it were to be judged, the lentil would be considered shy.

Typically, I make lentils before I am even ready to detail how I will use them. They are a preparation as often as they are an ingredient. They serve wonderfully as a base for vegetables and fish, for herbs and greens, for salads and sauces. I make lentil soup nearly every weekend. I am always surprised that it is such a favorite, but it is the soup that gets the most requests. It goes with everything, it loves company, it is a wonderful protein, a gentle ally, and a durable food, good for the heart, and filled with fiber.

Experiment a bit with the different kinds of lentils. The green and brown lentils— the French le Puy or the Italian *lenticchie verdi*—are the sturdiest for holding their shape and texture. The smaller black beluga, so like caviar in appearance, will stand out for its shape and color. And the red lentils that are split and hulled are the easiest to cook to a smooth consistency, for they soften more quickly without their hull.

There are records of people harvesting lentils as a food staple thirteen thousand years ago. That allows time for a lot of recipes. Here are some that I hope will lead you to the many places you can go with lentils.

Lentils Dressed with Croutons
and Fresh Parmesan

1½ cups (235 g) cooked
lentils, preferably le Puy
(see page 236)

½ cup (100 g) homemade
chicken or vegetable stock
(see pages 35–36)

Juice of ½ lemon

¾ cup (40 g) finely chopped fresh
flat-leaf parsley

Sea salt

1 teaspoon fresh oregano or
thyme leaves

2 to 3 cups (60 to 90 g)
homemade croutons (see
page 57), still hot

½ cup (50 g) freshly grated
Parmigiano-Reggiano cheese

1 tablespoon extra-virgin olive oil

Fresh ground black pepper

SERVES 4

**Lentils are the best handymen in the world. They are happy to work
in front, by themselves, or in back, with rice or pasta. Here is a
combination that always surprises me with its flavor. The lentils are
warm, the croutons are hot and crispy, the cheese soft and cool; it will
all be very smart.**

In a small pot, warm the lentils, adding and stirring the stock to mix.

When the lentils are fully heated, add the lemon juice, parsley, and
some salt and toss them together. Stir in the oregano.

Add half the croutons to the lentils and mix again. Spoon the lentils into
warm shallow bowls and add a good handful of Parmesan cheese.

Toss more of the croutons on top and then add the rest of the grated
Parmesan cheese. Finish with a stream of the olive oil and several grinds
of pepper. Add a little salt at the end.

Lentil Soup with Rice and Hot Italian Sausage

3 cups (720 ml) Lentil Soup
(page 236)

3 cups (720 ml) homemade
chicken stock (page 35)

½ cup (95 g) Arborio rice

Sea salt

¼ cup (60 ml) extra-virgin
olive oil

2 hot or mild Italian sausages,
cut into 1- to 2-inch (2.5- to
5-cm) pieces

1 teaspoon tomato paste

¼ cup (13 g) chopped fresh
flat-leaf parsley

Fresh ground black pepper

1 tablespoon dry white wine

2 tablespoons cold, unsalted
butter

¼ cup (25 g) freshly grated
Parmigiano-Reggiano cheese

SERVES 4

**Lentils are always pleased to accommodate rice, so I will often
toss a couple of tablespoons of Arborio rice into the lentils as they
are cooking. In this case, you are literally making space for the
rice to cook and then adding the sausage. It makes a quiet meal of
the process. The rice extends the lentils, adding its own texture, a
different aroma, and a new color as they cook together.**

In a saucepan, combine the lentil soup and 2 cups of the stock. Bring
to a boil over medium heat, then add the rice and a good pinch of salt
and stir. Adjust the heat to maintain a light boil. In a small pot, bring the
remaining stock to a simmer.

Heat a sauté pan over medium heat. Add the olive oil and sausages
and brown them well, 5 to 6 minutes. Smear the tomato paste into the
pan and loosen it with a little of the remaining chicken stock. Stir well,
scraping up any browned bits from the bottom of the pan. Let this bubble
a minute, adding a little of the parsley and some grinds of pepper.

Stir the lentils, checking to make sure the rice is not sticking. Add more
stock if needed.

Add the wine to the sausage and let it cook off. Add the butter to
thicken the pan sauce. Use a little chicken stock if it is too thick. It
needs to be silky beneath the sausage.

The rice should be done in 20 minutes. When it is soft but still has the
slightest bite to it, stir and turn off the heat below the lentils and the
rice. Taste and adjust the seasoning.

Ladle the soup into warm bowls. Carefully lay the sausage atop the soup
and pour some of the pan sauce across them. Top with the cheese and a
good sprinkle of the remaining parsley.

Lentils on Pita Bread

1 red bell pepper

Extra-virgin olive oil

1 hot Italian sausage

1 to 2 cups (200 to 400 g)
cooked lentils, preferably
le Puy (see page 236),
at room temperature

½ cup (120 ml) plain Greek
yogurt

¼ cup (5 g) chopped arugula

¼ cup (10 g) chopped fresh
cilantro

3 garlic cloves, minced

Juice of 1 lemon

Sea salt and fresh ground black
pepper

1 dried red chile, chopped

1 ripe avocado

Juice of 1 lime

2 medium tomatoes, peeled
and chopped

6 to 8 pitas (page 54) or tortillas

½ cup (120 ml) hummus

6 scallions, roots and stems
trimmed

SERVES 4

This is more a direction than a hard-and-fast recipe; you can tailor it to your tastes. There is a neighborly quality to lentils. They love to help, and here they serve as a wonderful base.

Preheat the oven to 400°F (205°C). Rub the bell pepper with olive oil and put it and the sausage into a small roasting pan. Roast for 35 to 40 minutes, until they are both darkened and the pepper is soft.

In a medium bowl, mix the lentils, half the yogurt, and a good pinch each of the arugula, cilantro, and garlic. Pour a little of the lemon juice on top, plus some salt and pepper. In a separate small bowl, stir together the remaining yogurt and a little more of the garlic. Set both aside.

Heat a sauté pan over medium heat. Add a little olive oil, the chile, a pinch more of the garlic, and the scallions. They should sizzle a bit, so turn them often. When they soften and some parts have blackened, 4 to 5 minutes, they are done. Turn the heat off. Once they have cooled, roughly slice them into ½-inch (12-mm) pieces, adding salt and black pepper to them.

Make a quick guacamole: Halve the avocado, remove the pit, and scoop the flesh into a small bowl. Add some of the lime juice, cilantro, a little minced garlic, and a pinch of salt. Mix and mash it a bit with a fork.

Take the bell pepper and the sausage out of the oven. Put the bell pepper in a small bowl and cover it with plastic wrap. In 10 minutes or so, the outer skin will loosen. Peel the pepper, halve it, and remove and discard the stem, ribs, and seeds. Lay the flesh flat on a cutting board. Cut it into strips. Split the sausage lengthwise and chop it into small pieces. Mix it in a small bowl with the red pepper strips, some salt and pepper, the remaining garlic, and some olive oil. Stir them together.

Salt the tomatoes, and then mix in some cilantro and a little lime juice and let them set.

You must heat the pitas—lay them right on the racks in the oven. Once the pitas are hot, layer the ingredients as follows: a little hummus, a tablespoon of lentils, some tomatoes, guacamole, sausage and peppers, scallions, a teaspoon of yogurt, a thin line of olive oil, and tosses of cilantro and arugula. Finish with a few drops of the lemon juice.

Lentil Soup with Broccoli Rabe in the Orecchiette

4 cups (960 ml) Lentil Soup
   (page 236)

Sea salt

5 to 6 ounces (140 to 170 g)
   good-quality dried orecchiette
   pasta

½ pound (225 g) broccoli rabe,
   ends trimmed, rinsed well

¼ cup (60 ml) extra-virgin
   olive oil

1 garlic clove, finely chopped

Pinch of red pepper flakes

Fresh ground black pepper

½ cup (50 g) freshly grated
   mixed Parmigiano-Reggiano
   and Pecorino Romano

2 tablespoons cold, unsalted
   butter

¼ cup (13 g) chopped fresh
   flat-leaf parsley

SERVES 4

This is a lovely dish: The lentils hold the ground, the orecchiette stick up like small clamshells, and the broccoli rabe brings the color.

It is a fine pasta shape, orecchiette—a small, ear-like shape, after the Italian word _orecchio_. Typically, it must be cooked longer than other pastas, sometimes for 18 to 20 minutes. Be sure to use some of the pasta water afterward; it is rich with the starch and flavor of the pasta.

In a medium pot, bring the soup to a simmer.

Bring a large pot of water to a boil. Add a good pinch of salt and the pasta. Plan to have the pasta cooked just as the broccoli rabe is finished being sautéed (it does not like standing around). Typically, I will start the pasta, noting the time it will need, and then expect the broccoli rabe to be done in 6 minutes or so.

Cut the broccoli rabe into 1- to 2-inch (2.5- to 5-cm) pieces and set aside.

Heat a sauté pan over medium heat. Add the olive oil, garlic, and red pepper flakes. As soon as the garlic begins to color, add the broccoli rabe, starting first with the pieces from the stalk end and then the florets and the leaves. Add a good pinch of salt and stir well.

When the broccoli has coated itself with the oil, add a tablespoon or two of the pasta water. Keep the heat up and toss and stir the broccoli until slightly softened, 3 to 4 minutes. Taste and adjust the seasoning. It should have a slight bitterness and a little fire from the pepper.

Drain the pasta, reserving some of the cooking water. Add the pasta to the pan with the broccoli rabe and toss well to get the pasta completely enmeshed with the broccoli. Add some black pepper, some of the grated cheese, and a little of the pasta water.

Stir the lentil soup, add the butter and a little of the pasta water to it, and stir to combine. Ladle the soup into warms bowls, sprinkle some cheese over the surface, and then lay a serving spoon full of the pasta and broccoli rabe mixture lightly on top.

Finish each serving with more cheese, a little black pepper, and the parsley.

Lentils with Roasted Chicken, Feta, and Sweetened Red Onion

1 medium red onion, thinly sliced

Sea salt

1 tablespoon red wine vinegar

6 tablespoons (90 ml) extra-virgin olive oil

Pinch of sugar

Fresh ground black pepper

1 cup (200 g) le Puy or Castelluccio lentils

2 bone-in, skin-on organic chicken breasts, about ¾ pound (340 g)

1 small carrot, finely chopped

1 yellow onion, finely chopped

1 celery stalk, finely chopped

1 leek, rinsed well and finely chopped

1 garlic clove

1 bay leaf

½ cup (75 g) crumbled feta

4 sprigs fresh thyme

½ lemon

SERVES 4

This is a fine dish, subtler and better versed than it might seem. The vegetables and the garlic flavor the lentils and make a wide bed for the chicken and the crumbled feta. The onions add their own freshness.

Soak the red onion in a bowl of cold water for 10 minutes, then rinse the onions, add fresh water and some salt, and let this soak for 20 minutes more. Drain the onion slices, rinse them with cold water, and dry with a paper towel. Dry the bowl in which they soaked and return them to the bowl. Add the vinegar, 2 tablespoons of the olive oil, the sugar, and some salt and pepper. Set aside.

Soak the lentils in cold water for 10 minutes, then drain.

Cook the two chicken breasts as directed in the Last Chicken Noodle Soup (page 227). Make and save ½ cup of the gravy and keep the chicken and gravy where it will stay warm.

Cook the lentils. Heat a heavy medium saucepan. Add the remaining olive oil, then the carrot, onion, celery, and leek and cook, stirring, for 5 minutes, until they have softened. Add the lentils, whole garlic, and bay leaf and cook for 5 minutes more, until you feel the lentils starting to stick. Add enough warm water (or stock, if you have it) to cover the lentils by 1 inch (2.5 cm). Stir, turn the heat down to low, and cook for about 40 minutes, until the lentils have softened but are not mushy. If the lentils look dry, add a little more water. Remove from the heat. If there is any liquid left in the pan, drain the lentils and then return them to the pan. Discard the bay leaf and garlic. Season the lentils with salt and pepper.

Serve a good portion of the lentils onto each warmed plate, leaving a soft pillow at the center.

Using a fork and small sharp knife, detach the chicken breasts from the bones beneath, and cut each breast crosswise into three pieces. Lay one or two pieces on each plate. Spoon the gravy over the pieces and onto the plate. Leave some of the lentils uncovered.

Give the onions a last toss in their dressing. Lay three or four marinated onion rings on top of the chicken on each plate. Sprinkle the feta cheese across the surface, add a sprig of thyme atop the chicken, and finish with a quick squeeze of lemon and two grinds of fresh black pepper.

FIVE WAYS TO COOK

Couscous and/or Quinoa

Couscous and quinoa are two foods that are very new and very old. They each have histories that scroll back into food production four thousand years ago. They share an economy of place—each food has evolved from and survived semi-arid conditions, water shortages, and measured rainfall.

Couscous originates from North Africa. It is not a grain; it is a byproduct of a grain, a piece created from durum wheat. Quinoa is native to South America, and specifically to the pre-Columbian Andes civilization. It is also not a grain, but a seed, from a plant called goosefoot, a first cousin to spinach. Both couscous and quinoa are high in protein, and quinoa is gluten-free. In a culinary sense, they are each survivors.

Both foods are quite porous, a quality that makes them good partners for yogurt and feta cheese and herbs and greens.

They are also quite light, making them a perfect companion in a salad. You can surround them with avocados and radishes, tomatoes and olives, bread and onions and know they will not gum up the works.

The natural allies to both couscous and quinoa are lemons and limes, mint and cilantro, garlic and red onion, hot chiles and ground black pepper. They are each a spark to the gentle souls of the food.

I have combined them into a single section to highlight their similarities—and to honor their quite remarkable renaissance and spirit. In the storm of new food technologies, in the often-bewildering collection of modernist cooking, couscous and quinoa are an ancient sound that has gently and crucially been replayed.

Couscous or Quinoa with Pear, Walnut, and Feta

½ cup (50 g) walnuts

2 cups cooked couscous (360 g) or quinoa (400 g), at room temperature (see page 237)

Sea salt

Juice of 1 lemon

½ cup (25 g) chopped fresh flat-leaf parsley

1 cup (20 g) baby arugula, rinsed and spun dry

¼ cup (60 ml) extra-virgin olive oil

2 tablespoons plain Greek yogurt

3 ripe sweet pears, peeled and sliced into thin wedges

¼ pound (115 g) feta, crumbled and kept cool

SERVES 4

This dish is a nice way to acknowledge the hospitality of couscous and quinoa, both very gracious hosts. It is a vignette of textures and colors, and it is important that each element is honored and part of the whole. Serve this as a lunch or as part of a dinner.

Heat a small sauté pan over low heat. Stir the walnuts for 5 minutes, until lightly toasted. Transfer to a plate to cool.

Put the couscous or quinoa in a medium bowl. Add some salt, half the lemon juice, and half the parsley. Stir to combine. Fold in the arugula. Drizzle 2 tablespoons of the olive oil over it all. Gently lay this in a serving bowl with shallow sides.

In a separate bowl, stir together the yogurt, remaining lemon juice, and some salt. Spoon this mixture onto the center of the couscous mixture. Do not clean the bowl—the trace of yogurt and lemon will work perfectly with the pears and walnuts.

Put the pear slices, walnuts, and feta into the bowl that had held the yogurt. Stir gently one or two times and then lay the pieces casually around the yogurt and the couscous. Use a light touch; they should not appear to be mashed together. Add the rest of the olive oil, sprinkle with the rest of the parsley, and serve immediately.

Couscous to Carry in the Squash

1/4 cup (60 ml) homemade chicken stock (see page 35)

2 medium carrots, cut into chunks

1 pound (455 g) butternut squash, peeled, seeded, and diced

Sea salt and fresh ground black pepper

1 fresh peperoncino, seeded and thinly sliced

2 garlic cloves, crushed a bit

1/2 teaspoon Aleppo pepper

2 tablespoons extra-virgin olive oil, plus more for serving

2 cups (360 g) cooked couscous (steamed in chicken stock, if possible, see page 237)

2 tablespoons cold, unsalted butter

1/4 cup (25 g) freshly grated Parmigiano-Reggiano cheese

1/4 cup (25 g) freshly grated Pecorino Romano cheese

Juice of 1 lime

1/2 cup (20 g) chopped fresh cilantro

1/2 cup (25 g) chopped fresh flat-leaf parsley

SERVES 4

It is a good healthy sight: The roasted squash, a little brown from the heat, coming in, laid out on the couscous. The couscous loves to help. In the right circumstance, this can be a meal all of its own.

But you must be careful to not serve too much squash at one time— it can seem almost too heavy. Lure people to the squash first with smaller quantities and let them come back for more.

Preheat the oven to 425°F (220°C). In a small pot, bring the stock to a simmer.

Bring a medium saucepan of water to a boil. Add the carrots and cook for 3 minutes, then drain well. Transfer to a large bowl and add the squash, some salt and black pepper, the peperoncino, garlic, and Aleppo pepper. Add 1 tablespoon of the olive oil and stir to combine.

Turn the ingredients out into a roasting pan and get it in the oven. After 10 minutes, turn the vegetables, then roast for about 25 minutes more, until the squash is tender when poked with a fork.

When the squash is nearly ready, heat a sauté pan over medium heat. Add the remaining 1 tablespoon of the olive oil, and a minute later, add the couscous and stir. Add the stock—it should bubble a bit—and stir to get it into the couscous. When the stock has been absorbed by the couscous, add the butter. Taste and adjust the seasoning, and stir. Add a little of the cheeses and turn off the heat.

Lay the couscous gently into warmed bowls. Spoon the squash and carrots on top, give a squeeze of lime to each, and sprinkle with the cilantro and the parsley. Add more cheese, some black pepper, and a little stream of olive oil to finish.

Couscous in the Springtime

Sea salt

½ cup (70 g) fresh or thawed frozen peas

12 cherry tomatoes

½ cup (120 ml) extra-virgin olive oil

1 bunch spring onions, halved lengthwise

Fresh ground black pepper

1 garlic clove, crushed

3 cups (540 g) cooked couscous (see page 237)

½ cup (10 g) chopped arugula

¼ cup (13 g) chopped fresh mint leaves

Juice of 1 lemon

½ cup (25 g) chopped fresh flat-leaf parsley

SERVES 4

These vegetables are the perfect cast for couscous—the players of springtime. Couscous is such a lovely color, and even more so when you add the particulars of spring vegetables. This is a pleasant dinner when the weather suddenly warms.

Bring a small saucepan of water to a boil. Add a good pinch of salt and the peas and cook for 6 minutes. Drain well and set aside.

Meanwhile, soak the cherry tomatoes in cold water for 5 minutes. Drain.

Heat a cast-iron pan over medium-high heat. Add half the olive oil and toss in the onions, cut side down. When that side is well browned, turn the onions over, add salt and pepper, and throw in the cherry tomatoes and the garlic. Cook for 4 minutes more, then remove from the heat.

Transfer the onions to a cutting board and chop them into 1-inch (2.5-cm) pieces. Coarsely chop the garlic as well. Drop them into a large bowl, add the tomatoes, couscous, and a swig of the olive oil, and stir. Add the peas, then the arugula and mint. The lemon juice is next, followed by a little salt, the remaining olive oil, and some pepper.

The parsley finishes the dish. Stir some into the whole, but save some for garnishing the tops.

Serve at room temperature. If possible, present the couscous in wide, shallow white bowls—they will show off the meal.

Quinoa and Garlic Spinach

I cup (200 g) cooked white
or red quinoa (steamed in
chicken stock, if possible,
page 237)

I pound (455 g) fresh spinach,
well washed and stemmed

Sea salt

¼ cup (60 ml) extra-virgin
olive oil

I tablespoon finely chopped
garlic

Pinch of red pepper flakes

Fresh ground black pepper

I teaspoon fresh lemon juice

I tablespoon chopped fresh
cilantro

SERVES 4

There is some culinary tradition for smoothing creamed spinach, or pesto, or a soup, with a softened potato. In this recipe, the quinoa is used in the same way, but it creates a slightly different effect. The quinoa retains its appearance. The sautéed spinach wraps and winds itself within the quinoa.

I love spinach by itself, but when combined with the quinoa, it seems less isolated and more substantial. Also, it is a wonderful dish reheated the next day for lunch.

Bring the quinoa to room temperature.

Heat a large saucepan over medium heat. Add the spinach, a good pinch of salt, and a sprinkle of water. Stir until you see the heat begin to wilt the bottom leaves. Cover the pot, but stay close. If the spinach is very fresh, it will be done in 3 to 4 minutes.

When the spinach is soft, drain it in a fine-mesh sieve. Press gently on the spinach to get the moisture out. Then lay the spinach on a cutting board and chop it into smaller pieces (I make six cuts in one direction and six in the other direction).

Heat a sauté pan over medium heat. Add most of the olive oil, the garlic, and the red pepper flakes. Cook, stirring and being careful not to burn the garlic, until you can smell it, then add the chopped spinach and stir well. Cook 2 minutes, always stirring. Add the quinoa. With a wooden spoon, work the quinoa and spinach together. After a minute, turn off the heat and season with salt and black pepper. Add the lemon juice and the cilantro. Finish with the rest of the olive oil.

VARIATION: The spinach and quinoa make a wonderful base for sautéed wild mushrooms when mushrooms are in season. Both porcini and chanterelle, which grow around conifers and pine trees, sit handsomely on the quinoa. Sauté the mushrooms in oil and butter with a little chopped onion, and when they are done, lay them over the spinach and quinoa.

Quinoa Sautéed with Cauliflower, Chanterelles, Raisins, and Eggs

½ pound (225 g) cauliflower
   florets

¼ cup (60 ml) extra-virgin
   olive oil

I small shallot, finely chopped

Sea salt and fresh ground
   black pepper

2 tablespoons unsalted butter

½ pound (225 g) chanterelles,
   cut into 1-inch (2.5-cm) pieces

¼ cup (35 g) raisins, softened in
   warm water for 10 minutes
   and drained

2 cups (400 g) cooked white
   quinoa (page 237)

I teaspoon sesame oil

I large fresh organic egg, beaten

I tablespoon chopped fresh
   chives

SERVES 4

This is quite simple and surely refreshing: a bite of cauliflower, a few mushrooms, the sweetness of the raisins, and the earthiness of the quinoa.

It could be a meal of its own, but if the chanterelles are abundant, and lovely, I will serve this before dinner, in smaller portions. Arrange each plate to show off the ingredients and then sprinkle on the chives to show that each plate is ready. The quinoa and eggs keep it sprightly and colorful. Cauliflower and chanterelles are both at their best in the fall, and this dish ties them together.

Soak the cauliflower in a large bowl of cold water for 10 minutes, then drain well.

Bring a large saucepan of water to a boil. Add the cauliflower and cook for 4 to 5 minutes, until just soft, then drain well.

Heat a sauté pan over medium heat. Add the olive oil and shallot. Cook until the shallot colors a bit. Add the cauliflower and some salt and pepper, and stir to mix. Cook for 3 to 4 minutes, until the cauliflower pieces begin to brown, then add the butter and chanterelles. Stir well and cook for 3 to 4 minutes more to cook the mushrooms, adding a little warm water if the pan seems too dry. Stir in the raisins. Add the quinoa, stirring and letting it heat for 20 seconds.

Turn the heat down to low, make a well in the center of the pan, and add the sesame oil. Moments later, spoon in the beaten egg and stir. Recombine all the parts. Season with salt and pepper, and finish with the chives, scattered everywhere.

FIVE WAYS TO COOK
Spaghetti

I first learned about cooking spaghetti correctly from Cristina Mechelli. She was twelve years old and cooking pasta with her father in their home above Firenze. He asked her to taste the spaghetti that was cooking; she took a strand out with a long fork and said to him, "Perfect." She then quickly looked at their three guests from the States and said, quietly, to her father, "A minute more."

To love spaghetti—to love any pasta—you must love both how simple and how complicated it is. You must take it for granted at the very same time that you watch it like a hawk. I often give my favorite dried pasta (Rustichella d'Abruzzo) away as a gift for the holidays—and it never fails that someone will particularly notice the difference.

Dried pasta is made from wheat flour and water, a simple enough prospect, but, like precious stones, there are many grades to the wheat and many subtleties to cross. A proper pasta will use only the best durum wheat semolina, but it is an expensive and particular flour. You must trust that the customer will know and value the difference. By appearance, the pasta may look very similar to a pasta made from any wheat—it is by taste and texture that the differences mount up.

Fresh pasta adds even further variant elements—eggs and time. If you are buying fresh pasta, be certain that the maker is using fresh organic eggs and that the pasta is no more than a day old. Fresh pasta makers are a separate breed. They know there are a hundred corners that they could cut, and they know that few people will know the difference of one pasta from another. In a sense, they work for tradition alone—if you are not going to do this the right way, then do not bother. In general, if you want fresh pasta, then you must make it yourself at home.

Otherwise, do as most Italians will do and buy the durum wheat dried pasta. I use spaghetti more than half the time. I love how it looks on the plate, in its half-coil recline. It is not the best pasta for all sauces and certainly not for a bolognese or other such ragù. But for a tomato sauce or a light cream, for an olive oil and garlic sauce, then to me it must be spaghetti. It is a pleasure to set someone's plate with the pasta, then more sauce, and cheese, basil, and cracked pepper. It is the one pasta I will make when I am only cooking for myself. And it is a wonderful pasta for the next day, even if you have no way to reheat it. Let it warm to room temperature, add a little olive oil, and you will be surprised how good it can taste. Here are five of my favorite ways to enjoy spaghetti.

Cacio e Pepe

Sea salt

¾ pound (340 g) good-quality
   dried tonnarelli or spaghetti

2 tablespoons fresh Tellicherry
   peppercorns, plus more
   for serving

¼ pound (200 g) Pecorino
   Romano cheese, plus more
   for serving

Extra-virgin olive oil

SERVES 4

I love this dish—it depends on good, dry, black peppercorns, and good peppercorns are often the last detail to seem important. This dish is quick and strong, and it is easy, in a way, but it is also a little chubby, so you will not be making it every week.

In Seattle, Michael Easton, the owner of Il Corvo, makes the best fresh pasta in town and the best *cacio e pepe*, and one night he made it for twenty people and still had plenty of time and temper for telling stories. I asked him later what was the key and he said it was to heat the cracked fresh peppercorns in a hot, dry, cast-iron skillet. Here is the rest of it.

Bring a big pot of water to a boil. Add a good pinch of salt and throw in your pasta, stirring it at first to make sure all parts are loosed. Cook for 10 to 12 minutes, or as directed on the package, while you prepare the rest of the dish.

Roughly crack the peppercorns. Heat a small cast-iron skillet over medium heat. Put the cracked peppercorns into it and toast them for 2 to 3 minutes. This will bring out their heat.

While the peppercorns toast, grate the Pecorino Romano cheese as finely as possible. You want a very light, lovely pile of cheese that will melt at the first touch of heat—the lightest possible snow. You will need about 2 cups (200 g) of grated cheese.

Remove the peppercorns from the heat. Place them in in a bowl and add 1 tablespoon cold water to stop the heating. Put three-quarters of the grated cheese into a warmed serving bowl, add the cracked pepper, and stir together.

When the pasta is nearly done, pull off 1 cup (240 ml) of the pasta water and then quickly drain the pasta in a colander. Shake it to remove excess water and add it immediately to the bowl with the cheese and pepper. Toss and toss—you want the heat to melt the cheese, you need the ground pepper to mix, and you must end with a creamy consistency. Your adjustment tools are the hot pasta water and the grated cheese—add one to loosen and one to thicken. You can also add a very thin stream of olive oil as a last resort.

The Pecorino Romano is very salty, but you may still need to add sea salt or the pasta will taste flat. Quickly serve the pasta into warmed bowls, adding more fresh cracked pepper and finish with more cheese. Then, one last quick grind of *pepe*, to show.

Spaghetti and Ripe Tomatoes

Sea salt

2 pounds (910 g) ripe tomatoes

¾ pound (340 g) good-quality
   dried spaghetti

1 garlic clove, finely chopped

¼ cup (60 ml) extra-virgin
   olive oil

1 teaspoon tomato paste

Fresh ground black pepper

12 to 16 basil leaves, the smaller
   the better

½ cup (50 g) freshly grated
   Parmigiano-Reggiano

SERVES 4

If you cannot access good tomatoes, this recipe is not of much use. It relies on a good growing season and a good moment in time—the basil is up and you have more tomatoes than you have plans for. This is an easy way to enjoy the good fortune and to set a bar for the next time that summer arrives.

Bring a large pot of water to a boil. Add a good pinch of salt and drop the tomatoes into the pot. Blanch them for 10 seconds, then strain them out and transfer to a colander set over a bowl. Add the pasta to the boiling water and cook for 10 to 12 minutes, or as directed on the package. Taste after 10 minutes—you want it slightly underdone.

Meanwhile, cut the tomatoes in half right in the colander, being careful not to nip your colander, and slide the skins off. Then gently squeeze them to release the liquid and the seeds and put the meat on a cutting board. You can toss the liquid and seeds.

Cut the deseeded tomatoes into small pieces, put them in a bowl, and add the garlic, half the olive oil, the tomato paste, and a good sprinkling of salt and pepper. Stir to mix and add a few of the whole basil leaves.

Drain the pasta quickly and add it to the bowl with the sauce. Before you stir it together, salt the pasta. Add a thin line of olive oil and a small handful of the grated Parmesan. Then stir to combine it all. Take a taste: This recipe relies a bit on salt, so add another good pinch if it needs it.

As you serve the pasta, add the remaining olive oil and then the cheese. Finish with the remaining basil leaves and a final grind of pepper.

VARIATION: There are times that I want a more assertive fresh tomato sauce. Then I will sauté the garlic first in olive oil for 2 to 3 minutes over medium heat, add a pinch of red pepper flakes, and then add the chopped tomatoes. This I cook, uncovered, for 4 to 5 minutes, until the tomatoes soften. Then I add a 28-ounce (785-g) can of San Marzano tomatoes (not tomato paste). I mash and stir them well and let this bubble for 10 minutes.

When the spaghetti is nearly done, I drain it and add it directly to the pan. It will finish cooking with the sauce for 2 minutes, the starch from the pasta helping to thicken the tomato sauce. Then I add the Parmesan cheese, salt, black pepper, and basil leaves.

Spaghetti Frittata

1 tablespoon extra-virgin
olive oil

2 hot Italian sausages, cut into
1-inch (2.5-cm) pieces

Sea salt and fresh ground black
pepper

½ pound (225 g) good-quality
dried spaghetti

½ cup (70 g) fresh or thawed
frozen peas

2 tablespoons cold, unsalted
butter

½ cup (50 g) freshly grated
Parmigiano-Reggiano cheese,
plus more for serving

2 or 3 large fresh organic eggs,
cracked, at room temperature

½ cup (120 ml) heavy cream, at
room temperature

¼ cup (13 g) chopped fresh
flat-leaf parsley

SERVES 4

**Sometimes this is just the thing. It makes a small fuss out of two
Italian sausages and a couple of eggs. Try to remember the peas—
they stand out. This is great when served with a simple green salad
with a lemony dressing (page 73).**

Preheat the oven to 500°F (260°C). Bring a large pot of water to a boil
for the pasta.

Heat a 10-inch (25-cm) ovenproof sauté pan over medium heat for
a minute. Add the olive oil and sausage and cook until the sausage is
browned well on all sides, 6 to 8 minutes. Remove from the heat.

Drain the sausage pieces on a paper towel and salt and pepper them.
Pour off any fat in the pan but do not wash it—you are coming back to
it with the pasta.

When the water is boiling, add a good pinch of salt and then add the
pasta. Stir to make sure nothing sticks and cook for 10 to 12 minutes,
or as directed on the package. After 5 minutes, add the peas to the pot
as well, so they can cook with the pasta. Drain well.

Heat the sauté pan in which you cooked the sausage over medium heat.
Add the butter. When it begins to foam, add the sausage, scraping the pan
to smooth its surface and get any bits up. Add the pasta and peas, a good
pinch of salt, and a little cheese and stir gently. Remove from the heat.

In a small bowl, beat the eggs until smooth, then whisk in the cream,
parsley, and some salt and pepper. Pour the egg mixture over the
sausages and pasta. Sprinkle a little more cheese on top and put the pan
directly into the hot oven. Bake for no more than 5 minutes. It should
soufflé a bit, and even brown on top a touch.

Carefully bring it out of the oven. The frittata will lose most of its puff but
will still be a pleasure. Serve immediately, with additional cheese on the side.

Spaghetti and Soup

5 to 6 cups (1.2 to 1.4 L) soup broth, stock (see pages 35–36), or any thicker, pureed soup like white bean, lentil, or tomato

¼ cup (60 ml) extra-virgin olive oil

4 tablespoons (½ stick/55 g) cold, unsalted butter

1 shallot, finely chopped

1 tablespoon chopped pancetta or prosciutto

½ cup (25 g) fresh bread crumbs

Sea salt and fresh ground black pepper

1 garlic clove, finely chopped

Pinch of red pepper flakes

¼ pound (115 g) good-quality dried spaghetti, linguine, or bucatini

¼ cup (35 g) fresh or thawed frozen peas

½ cup (50 g) freshly grated Parmigiano-Reggiano (cow) or Pecorino Romano (sheep) cheese

½ cup (25 g) finely chopped fresh flat-leaf parsley

1 teaspoon fresh lemon zest

SERVES 4

This does not seem like the most difficult thing to do or think of—adding spaghetti to a soup. But I like it more than I remember to do it, and there are a few details that make it particularly good.

For the soup, you can use either a broth or a thicker, firmer soup, like a white bean, lentil, or bisque-like tomato soup. For both styles of soup, you could, of course, simply add pasta toward the end of its cooking cycle. The pasta, or rice, would be cooked by the slow boiling liquid and make itself a part of the soup, thickening and broadening the base. The classic version and reference would be *tortellini en brodo*, where the delicate shape of the pasta is brought alive by the soup.

But this is a different technique. You do not add the pasta until it has already been (mostly) cooked, sauced, and detailed. The pasta is added only the minute or so before serving the soup. It does not become part of the soup—it becomes partners with the soup, bringing its own colors, tastes, textures, and signals. It arrives like a chorus, claiming not to be the lead voice but to be many voices.

It is a good meal and makes an envied lunch the next day. Heat the leftover soup quickly to avoid overcooking the noodles. You might even pull them out and return them to the soup only when it is hot again. Use freshly grated Parmesan to make the dish at least partly dressed just for the occasion.

In a medium pot, bring the stock or soup to a slow simmer. Bring a large pot of water to a boil for the pasta.

Heat a 10-inch (25-cm) sauté pan over medium heat for a minute. Add half the olive oil and half the butter. After a moment, add the shallot and pancetta. Stir well and often to brown the pancetta.

After 5 minutes or so, add the bread crumbs, some salt and black pepper, the garlic, and red pepper flakes, and stir. Let the bread crumbs brown a bit, 6 to 8 minutes. If the pan gets too hot, turn down the heat and stir.

Add a good pinch of salt and the dried pasta (see Note) to the pot of boiling water and stir.

When the pasta has come to a boil, add the peas and turn down the heat to maintain a slow boil. Cook the pasta until nearly done (it is going into a soup, so you don't want it cooked through), 10 minutes or a few minutes less than directed on the package. Drain it quickly, saving a little of the pasta cooking water. Transfer the pasta and peas to a warmed bowl and add a handful of the cheese and some salt and quickly stir it all well. Add the remaining butter and a few tablespoons of the pasta water and stir. Add half the bread crumb mixture to the bowl.

The pasta should be a little loose and gangly but not bone-dry and not sopping wet. Taste it—you have a lot of input from the cheese and the pancetta, so check if you need salt and pepper. Then add a little more of the bread crumbs and the cheese. Add some of the parsley and stir again.

Ladle your hot soup broth into warmed bowls, leaving a little room for the pasta, and taste it for saltiness. Then, with tongs, lay some of the pasta atop each bowl—enough to cover three-quarters of the surface but not so much that the balance will be lost. Top with a little of the remaining bread crumbs, Parmesan, parsley, and season with salt and pepper. Finish with a thin drizzle of olive oil and the lemon zest. The heat from the soup will loosen the pasta from below.

NOTE: You can certainly use fresh pasta but, if so, cook it after the bread crumbs have browned, for it will only need 2 to 3 minutes of cooking.

Spaghetti in the Springtime

½ pound (225 g) asparagus

½ pound (225 g) fresh fava beans in the pod, shelled

½ pound (225 g) fresh peas in the pod, shelled

Sea salt

½ pound (225 g) good-quality dried spaghetti

2 tablespoons extra-virgin olive oil

2 garlic cloves, thinly sliced

Fresh ground black pepper

1 bunch arugula (about 2 cups/ 40 g), rinsed and spun dry, stems removed

½ cup (50 g) freshly grated Parmigiano-Reggiano cheese, plus more for serving

4 tablespoons (½ stick/55 g) cold, unsalted butter, cut into three pats

SERVES 4

Sometimes, there is a dish that has a specific season. A simple pasta with asparagus, fava beans, and fresh peas is that kind of a dish. You can make it best in the spring, but you can only make it perfectly for about two weeks of that spring—the precise intersection of the three vegetables being at their freshest.

Bring a large pot of water to a boil for the pasta.

Trim 1 inch (2.5 cm) off the woody ends of the asparagus, rinse it under cold water, then transfer to a large bowl filled with cold water to soak for 3 to 5 minutes. Pull the asparagus out and let it drain—the short bath will help it cook faster, but a longer soak would only make it soggy.

Bring a medium pot of water to a boil for the peas and favas. When it comes to a boil, add a good pinch of salt. Fill a bowl with cold water and ice cubes and set it nearby. Boil the fava beans for 2 minutes only, then pull them out and plop them into the ice-water bath to stop the cooking. Do the same for the peas.

Squeeze each fava bean from one end between your thumb and fore-finger to remove the skin. The luscious, very green center should pop out the other end. Discard the skins. Lightly salt the beans and try not to eat them. Depending on freshness, dexterity, and quality control, the skinning can move quickly or slowly.

Fill a sauté pan wide enough to hold the asparagus with a couple of inches (5 cm) of fresh water and bring to a boil. Add a good pinch of salt and the asparagus, and let it boil rapidly. If the asparagus is thin, 1 minute will be plenty; if it is thick as a thumb, you may need a minute or two more. You are not cooking it through; you are simply setting it on the way. As an alarm, absolutely pull it out if suddenly you smell asparagus. Drain it well and let it sit on a warmed platter; be careful that there is no water pooling beneath, or the liquid will continue to soften the asparagus. Rinse the sauté pan quickly, dry it, and put it back near the stove, as you will do the rest of the cooking in this pan.

Cut the tips off the asparagus and set them aside. Cut the stalks on an angle into 2-inch (5-cm) lengths and set them aside separately. If the stalks are soft, then remember next time to take the asparagus out of the boiling water sooner! They should be firm enough to feel the cut.

Add a good pinch of salt to the pasta cooking water and throw in your pasta. Stir to make sure nothing sticks. Cook for 10 to 12 minutes, or as directed on the package.

Meanwhile, heat a sauté pan over medium heat. Add the olive oil and garlic and let that heat up, but not color, for a minute. When you can smell the garlic, add the asparagus stems (not the tips), then the fava beans and peas. Stir well to incorporate with the garlic and oil. Mush some of the peas with a wooden spoon to help thicken the sauce. Season with salt and pepper and keep tossing the mix. It is a very up-tempo sauté. You are not trying to brown anything; you are simply getting it well heated. Make sure the garlic does not brown. If the pan looks dry, add a tablespoon or so of the pasta cooking water. After 3 minutes, throw in a handful of arugula and stir to incorporate.

Taste the pasta. It can be slightly underdone, but it must be pulled and drained no more than 4 minutes after you have started to sauté or the vegetables will overcook. Drain the pasta, reserving some of the cooking water.

Add the still-wet pasta to the pan with the vegetables and give it a good stir. Add a pinch of salt, the asparagus tips, and a small handful of the cheese. Stir again and fold in the cold butter pats. The butter should melt, but you will still need to add a half ladle of pasta water to smooth it all out. Turn off the heat and add a second handful of arugula and a little more cheese. Taste and adjust the seasoning, and add at least a few cracks of black pepper.

Serve in warmed bowls. Here is how you want it to look: The pasta should be at the base, amused but disheveled, and not at all weighty. The asparagus, fava beans, and peas are the divas, the arugula is a gentle support, and the asparagus tips should be the most glamorous and independent of all the players. The cheese is a kind of glitter—the dish a lovely show of spring's best ensemble.

PROTEIN

Five Ways to Bring the Beasts, Birds, and Fish to Dinner

The preparations in this chapter range from the careful details of a roast chicken to the four-minute grilling of lamb top round. They share many things, but none more crucial than technique. They are an example of using what is possible in the best possible way. You can use the basic methods offered here in combination with many of the preceding recipes, pairing the steak, fish, chicken, or lamb with a vegetable, a couscous, or a pasta.

There is a quiet economy to these five dishes. They each take some advantage and then proudly move ahead to make their best presentation.

Lamb Thigh with Couscous and Tomatoes

2 cups (360 g) cooked couscous (see page 237)

1 trimmed lamb thigh, about 1 pound (455 g)

Sea salt and fresh ground black pepper

4 tablespoons (60 ml) extra-virgin olive oil

1 shallot, minced

2 garlic cloves, crushed

12 to 16 cherry tomatoes

4 sprigs fresh thyme

2 tablespoons cold, unsalted butter

½ cup (20 g) chopped fresh cilantro

1½ lemons

½ cup (120 ml) plain Greek yogurt

Fresh mint sprigs

SERVES 2 TO 3

You will not see this cut very often. It is part of the lamb leg, above the shank—the muscle that crosses the front of the thigh. And you will never see it at holidays. They want to sell the whole leg of lamb then. But it is otherwise available. Butchers might label it "top round." It is shaped like a flank steak. A good butcher will know the cut. The one difficulty can be trimming the piece, if the butcher has not (it should have been done). It will have a hard outer layer of fat and some silver membrane that need to be trimmed away before you grill it. You can pair it with any number of accompaniments, but this is my favorite. You are slightly cooking the shallot, browning the garlic, rushing the tomatoes, and adding the couscous—all to set a place for the lamb.

Bring the couscous and lamb to room temperature. Generously salt and pepper the lamb.

Heat a sauté pan on medium high for 2 minutes—then add 2 tablespoons of the olive oil and swirl the pan to coat. In a minute or so, the pan should be smoking a little. Add the lamb. Cook for 2 minutes on one side, turn it, and then cook it a minute or so on the other side and the lamb should be done. Take a peek by cutting a slit at the middle—if it seems too raw, put it back on the heat and let it sear for another minute, but be cautious to not overcook. Let the meat rest on a warm plate.

Heat a sauté pan over medium heat. Add the rest of the olive oil, the shallot, and garlic and sauté for 4 minutes. Add some salt and pepper. Toss in the cherry tomatoes, thyme, and 1 tablespoon water to create a little steam. Swirl the pan so the tomatoes roll about and cook for 1 minute. Add the couscous and butter and stir well with a rubber spatula. Cook for a minute more, then add some of the cilantro. Remove from the heat, taste, and adjust the seasoning.

Spoon the couscous sauté into warmed bowls. Empty the sauté pan and squeeze 1 lemon onto the pan's surface. If it has cooled too much, set it over low heat, just enough to help the lemon juice deglaze the pan. Very quickly add the yogurt, swirl to mix once, and take the pan off the heat.

Spoon a little of the yogurt atop the couscous. Sprinkle the rest of the cilantro over the top and add some pepper.

Slice the lamb against the grain on an angle, spritz with the remaining lemon, and serve on a platter garnished with sprigs of mint.

Monkfish Roasting

1 to 1½ pounds (455 to
680 g) fresh monkfish tail, blue
membrane removed

Sea salt and fresh ground black
pepper

¼ cup (60 ml) extra-virgin
olive oil

4 or 5 sprigs fresh thyme or
rosemary (optional)

2 tablespoons cold, unsalted
butter

¼ cup (13 g) chopped fresh
flat-leaf parsley

1 lemon

SERVES 4

Monkfish is a little like the lamb thigh. They are both slightly outsiders. And they both take a little work—not on your part, but on the part of the butcher or fishmonger—for these proteins need a little trimming to become presentable. But then, they are both wonderful. They love a little attention.

It is said that monkfish has a taste and texture that is somewhat like lobster. It is firm and muscular—and it can sit, quite by itself, on the plate, with a little lemon juice, parsley, and butter for company. When you buy monkfish, you must be certain it is as fresh as possible. Serve it with a plain salad and fresh bread to catch some of the juices.

Pat the monkfish dry with paper towels. Lay the fish in a stainless-steel bowl and salt and pepper it well. Cover the bowl and refrigerate for 1 hour. This will season the fish and help draw out a little moisture.

Preheat the oven to 425°F (220°C).

Bring the fish out 10 minutes before you intend to cook it. Pat it dry again with paper towels and rub the fish all over with some of the olive oil.

Heat an ovenproof sauté pan over medium heat. Add the remaining olive oil and, a minute later, when the oil is hot, add the monkfish.

Turn the fish after a minute or so, then turn again, crack some pepper over it, add the thyme (if using), and put the pan in the oven. Cook until the flesh is firm and white, 7 minutes or so; check on the fish after 5 minutes. (If you cook it too long, the flesh will start to flake apart.) Immediately add the butter and a little parsley to the pan and squeeze some lemon juice on top.

Let the fish rest for 4 minutes before you serve it.

Slive into 4 pieces. Lay the fish on warmed plates and pour the juices from the pan all over each piece. Season with a little salt and garnish with the remaining parsley and a little more lemon.

Hanger Steak with Avocado and Broccoli and Rice Sauté

2 pounds (910 g) hanger steak, typically 2 pieces

Sea salt and fresh ground black pepper

¼ cup (13 g) chopped fresh flat-leaf parsley

¼ cup (60 ml) extra-virgin olive oil, plus more as needed

½ pound (225 g) broccoli

2 garlic cloves, thinly sliced

1 dried red chile

1 red bell pepper, cut into strips

1 cup (175 g) cooked rice (see page 235)

½ cup (10 g) arugula, rinsed and spun dry

2 ripe avocados, sliced and sprinkled with lemon, salt, and pepper

SERVES 4

Every generation has their particular corners of economy and adjustment, especially in regard to food. There was a time that Chilean sea bass was practically unknown and unloved. It was a fish that the captain and crew ate, but no one purchased. Hanger steak and lamb thighs are like that. They are both the butcher's favorites, but for years, they were hard to find—no one knew or cared about them. You can find them now, and soon enough their prices may even go up.

I will often pick up a hanger steak or two on my way home from work and make up a meal around it once I get home. They are quick and versatile and can be cooked in or out of doors. They like improvisation.

I will serve it with broccoli, a little spice, and a base of lovely steamed rice. I add some arugula to bring even more support to the taste of the vegetables. But if I am short on time, I may skip the rice and simply serve the steak with some avocado and a simple salad and be done.

Dry the hanger steak with a paper towel. Salt and pepper it very well and bring it to room temperature for 20 minutes or so before cooking. If you are using an outdoor grill, get it hot. If you are cooking indoors, preheat the oven to 450°F (230°C). A hanger steak needs heat to cook properly.

To grill the hanger steak, lay it on the hottest section of the fire and turn it as each side darkens. It should take 5 to 6 minutes per side, or a total of 10 to 12 minutes, to firm up. Let it stand for 10 minutes and then sprinkle with salt and the parsley.

If cooking indoors, heat a cast-iron pan over medium-high heat. Add some olive oil, and when it smokes, add the hanger. Turn it a couple of times until the sides are dark, about 2 to 3 minutes, and then put the pan in the oven for about 10 minutes to finish. Push on the meat with a forefinger—when it has firmed, it is done. The pieces should be near black on the outside, but quickly pink within.

Add a little more cracked pepper to the steak. Let it stand for 10 minutes.

Meanwhile, trim the dried end of the broccoli stalk and peel the outer skin from it. Soak the broccoli in a large bowl of cold water for 5 minutes.

Bring a big pot of water to a boil. Add a good pinch of salt. Drop the broccoli into the boiling water and cook until you can pierce the stalk with a fork. If it is very fresh, it might be done in 2 minutes. In any case, do not cook longer than 4 minutes. Drain it quickly.

Heat a sauté pan over medium heat. Add the olive oil, garlic, chile, and a little salt. Give the pan a shake.

Quickly chop the broccoli into 2-inch (5-cm) pieces and get them all into the sauté pan. Stir to combine—it should be lively. Keep stirring for a couple of minutes, then add the bell pepper and, a moment later, the rice. The rice will quickly want to stick. Stir to combine well and then, suddenly, turn off the heat, add some salt and black pepper, and let it rest for a minute. Taste it—it should be a little spicy and hot and unruly.

Stir in the arugula and then divide among warmed plates. Slice the hanger steak against the grain on an angle and serve on a platter with the avocado and some salt just to the side. Pour any juices over the sliced meat.

Roasted Chicken

SERVES 4

1 (3- to 4-pound/1.4- to 1.8-kg) whole organic chicken

¼ cup (60 ml) extra-virgin olive oil, plus more for the pan

Sea salt and fresh cracked black pepper

1 lemon

2 sprigs fresh rosemary

2 garlic cloves, very thinly sliced

½ cup (120 ml) homemade chicken or vegetable stock (see pages 35–36), plus more as needed

1 to 2 teaspoons all-purpose flour

2 tablespoons dry white wine

2 tablespoons cold, unsalted butter, cut into cubes

½ cup (25 g) chopped fresh flat-leaf parsley

The hardest part about roasted chicken is getting a good chicken. Once you have found a good, organic chicken, you can proceed with a few specific details and know that you are on higher ground.

Pat the chicken dry and bring it to room temperature (see Note).

Preheat the oven to 425°F (220°C). Rub a roasting pan with a light film of olive oil.

Season the chicken well, inside and out, with salt and pepper. Rub the bird's every surface with the olive oil. Roll the lemon to soften it and stuff the whole lemon and rosemary in the cavity with some salt and pepper. Tuck the garlic under the skin wherever it is loose and even smear a little salt in there with the garlic.

Lay the bird in the prepared roasting pan (see Note), breast side down and with the back upright, and grind a little more pepper onto the back surface of the chicken.

Roast for 20 minutes, then bring the bird out and flip it right side up, being careful to loosen any skin that might be stuck to the pan. Baste the bird with pan juices and get it back into the oven, turning the oven temperature down to 400°F (205°C). Roast for 40 to 50 minutes more, depending on size and freshness. During that time, baste the chicken with the pan juices at least three times more. Do the basting carefully but quickly, so you do not lose the oven heat.

The bird is done when its internal temperature is about 165°F (75°C), but you will, in truth, smell that it is close. After some experience, the smell will be near as accurate for you as the thermometer, and that will help you keep track of things. As they say, trust your intuition, a little.

Transfer the chicken to a warmed serving platter, pouring any liquid that has collected in the bird's cavity back into the roasting pan. Cover the chicken lightly with aluminum foil and let it rest for 10 to 15 minutes.

In a small pot, bring the stock to a simmer.

Now to make a simple gravy: Pour off and discard at least half of the pan liquid. Some birds will throw very little liquid—it is the surface fat that you do not need all of. The fat will have risen to the surface, so pour slowly to save the good juices and bits below the fat.

Set the pan on the stovetop over low heat and sprinkle a teaspoon or so of flour over the surface of the pan juices. Stir and let the flour brown just a touch as it mixes with the juices. Then add some hot stock, stirring into the corners and beneath whatever might have stuck to the surface in the roasting. Keep adding liquid if need be—you want the gravy to bubble slowly for 8 to 10 minutes, as it brings up and incorporates all the stuck parts and the juices. Once the gravy seems to have smoothed everything together, add the wine and stir. A minute later, add the butter and stir as the butter melts and binds the sauce. As soon as the butter has melted, you are done. Taste the gravy, adjust the seasoning, and toss some parsley atop it all.

Transfer the gravy to a warmed bowl or measuring cup and set it aside so it will not lose heat. You can add a little hot liquid if it seems to thicken too much. Protect the gravy—it is the crucial softener to the meat of the chicken, but also the binder to whatever else is being served. It is the hand holder, bringing all the separate parts together. Later, if you are making soup from the bones, the leftover gravy will be the perfect final taste to add to the soup.

Using a sharp knife, cut the wings, legs, and thighs off the bird. Then, with the tip of the knife, cut one of the breasts off, doing your best to keep it intact, and lay it cut side down on a board. Cut across the breast to make three or four even pieces. Repeat with the other breast.

Serve the bird by placing a wing, thigh, or leg on each plate next to a few pieces of breast meat. Finish with the gravy, some more parsley, and some pepper.

NOTE: One hour before you plan to cook the bird, bring it out of the refrigerator and let it come to room temperature. Pat it dry one last time with paper towels, especially around the legs and the back.

Make sure to find the right roasting pan. It must be firm enough to not wobble, it must have a rim so the juices do not run onto your hand or the oven, but the rim must be no higher than an inch (2.5 cm) or so, or the heat will not circulate, and the bird will steam more than roast. Also, the pan must be able to sit on the stovetop, so you can make the gravy. You can use a low-sided sauté pan if it will fit in the stove and the handle is ovenproof.

Hot Italian Sausage with Pasta

3 Italian hot sausages (about
 1 pound/455 g)

2 tablespoons extra-virgin olive
 oil, plus more for drizzling

1 (28-ounce/785-g) can San
 Marzano tomatoes

Sea salt and fresh ground
 black pepper

4 to 6 fresh plum tomatoes (or
 any fresh tomato)

2 garlic cloves, finely chopped

1 dried hot red chile

1 loose cup (about 40 g) fresh
 basil leaves, then lightly
 chopped or torn

1 pound (455 g) good-quality
 dried pasta, such as tagliatelle
 or linguine

½ cup (50 g) freshly grated
 Pecorino Romano cheese
 or Parmigiano-Reggiano and
 Pecorino Romano, plus more
 as needed

SERVES 4

**If you can find fresh basil, if you have some tomatoes that need to be
used, if you can get some good Italian sausage, this is a particularly
handy recipe.**

Bring a medium pot of water to a boil. Fill a bowl with ice water.

Cut the sausages into 1-inch (2.5-cm) chunks. Do not worry if they are
a little imprecise.

Heat a large sauté pan over medium heat for 20 seconds. Add the olive
oil and sausage chunks and stir to coat. Brown the sausage on all sides,
4 to 6 minutes.

Pour the canned tomatoes with their juices into a bowl. With clean
hands, crush the tomatoes into smaller pieces. Pour the tomatoes into
the pan with the sausage. Stir to combine. Add some salt and black
pepper.

Slide the fresh tomatoes into the boiling water and let them roll for 1
minute. Look for the tiniest softening of the tomato skin, then pull the
tomatoes out with a slotted spoon and drop them into the ice-water
bath. Peel and seed the tomatoes, then chop the flesh and drop it into
the pan with the sausage mixture.

Add the garlic and chile to the pan. Stir well to combine and adjust the
temperature to maintain a gentle simmer. Add half the basil and stir again.
You will now, for the most part, leave the sauce to its own progress. You
need only keep track that it does not stick. If it thickens too much, add
some of the pasta cooking water and stir. Let the sauce gently simmer,
uncovered, for 25 to 30 minutes. Taste it for salt and pepper.

After the sauce has been cooking for 20 minutes or so, bring a large pot
of water to a boil. Add 1 tablespoon of salt and the pasta and stir to
make sure nothing is sticking. Cook according to the package directions,
draining the pasta a minute before the recommended time.

Pour the drained, still-wet pasta into the sauce. Mix it well—it will
still be bubbling, so you will need to stay close. Add salt, a little of the
cheese so it can stick to the pasta, and after a minute, turn off the heat.
The sauce will have thickened from the pasta starch.

Serve in warmed bowls and finish each with more cheese, black pepper,
and basil leaves. At the end, lay a slight line of olive oil across each plate.

WEEKEND COOKING

Five Preparations That Take a Little Time

It need not be a weekend. You can make any of these dishes with a free afternoon. They take a little fussing and care, in either the shopping or the preparation. And they each can use a little attention while they are cooking.

But they are all good-hearted, pleased to help, and pleased to linger. It is the details that make them welcome. Some are perfect for a celebratory end-of-week meal and some are even more welcome by the next day, and can help set up the week to come.

Sauce Bolognese

2 pounds (910 g) ground beef, or
  1 pound (455 g) ground beef
  and 1 pound (455 g) ground
  pork, at room temperature

Sea salt and fresh ground black
  pepper

¼ cup (60 ml) extra-virgin
  olive oil

1 carrot, minced

1 medium onion, finely chopped

1 celery stalk, finely chopped

1 bay leaf

2 sprigs fresh rosemary

1 cup (240 ml) milk

1 cup (240 ml) beef or
  homemade chicken stock
  (see page 35) or hot water, or
  more if needed

½ cup (120 ml) red or white
  wine (see Note)

¼ teaspoon freshly grated
  nutmeg

1 (28-ounce/785-g) can San
  Marzano tomatoes

1 garlic clove, finely chopped

½ pound (225) good-quality
  dried pasta, such as penne, ziti,
  or fusilli

½ cup (50 g) freshly grated
  Parmigiano-Reggiano cheese

¼ cup (13 g) chopped fresh
  flat-leaf parsley

SERVES 4 TO 6

A Bolognese sauce is a wonderful economy. For the price of a rib-eye steak, you can make a serving for six. It is your labor and attention that make the meal. You are the force making ground beef elegant.

There are countless shortcuts to a sauce like this. There is even the sense that anything that cooks slowly, for five hours, need not take its particulars too seriously, nor itself. Personally, I like the details to this recipe. To my tastes, they are true. But they slow up the early work. Once you do get the sauce to its slow simmer, you have most of the five hours' cooking time back.

Bolognese sauce is particular about temperatures. The meat being at room temperature, the milk being hot, the stock being warm, the pan not burning the vegetables or the meat, the simmer being a slow, slight bubble. Keep track of these matters; they are the difference, and the difference will show up five hours later. Choose a wide, heavy-bottomed pan, stainless steel or enameled cast iron. If you used a thin-bottomed pan, the heat will be too sharp and the ingredients will be more likely to burn. Once you find the right pan, you will always make this sauce in it.

As is true of anything cooked for a length of time, the sauce will be even better the next day. Once refrigerated, you can easily skim any fat from the surface. That said, I have never made sauce Bolognese and not eaten at least some of it the day I cooked it.

The sauce freezes perfectly. It is, in a way, the subtlest quick dinner solution, a kind of in-house takeout. Pull the sauce from the freezer, heat a pot of water, grate some Parmesan, chop a little parsley or basil, heat the bowls, and you are nearly there.

I have added Bolognese to my risottos, stirred it gladly into fresh pappardelle, added fresh wild mushrooms to it, and rolled tortellini in its sauce for an elegant first course. You have done the work; you have the right to enjoy its pleasures. Serve it with a tubular pasta as a fine sample or appetizer. If you want to serve it as dinner, simply double the amount of pasta to a full pound.

Season the meat with salt and pepper.

Heat a heavy-bottomed pan over medium-high heat. Add the olive oil, then the carrot, onion, celery, bay leaf, and rosemary and stir. Cook for 5 to 6 minutes. Do not let the vegetables burn—you must stay close and stir. It is a lively process, this sauce, until it is ready for its long, slow simmer.

Add the meat, arranging it a little so the vegetables step aside and the meat is right against the bottom of the hot pan. You need to sear it— not scorch it or brown it. Let it sit, untouched, for 5 minutes. Then stir it all well, mixing the vegetables into the meat, and cook for 10 minutes, stirring for this stretch to get all the meat heated and cooked through.

In a small pot, bring the milk to a simmer. In another pot, bring the stock to a simmer.

When ground meat starts to stick to the pan's surface, it is time to add the wine. Mix well and let the wine cook away to nothing, 10 minutes or so, about the time you again feel the meat sticking to the bottom. Add the hot milk. Stir quickly and turn the heat down to low. Let the mixture bubble for 20 minutes, until the milk, too, seems to be gone. Add the nutmeg while the milk is sweetening the beef, and keep stirring.

Pour the tomatoes and their juices into a stainless-steel bowl. With clean hands, lightly crush the tomatoes. Pour them into the pan with the meat mixture and stir, being careful to stir along the sides and the bottom of the pan to get everything ready for the long simmer. Add the garlic at this time, as the tomatoes will protect it from burning. Bring the mixture to a slow boil—raise the heat a bit if you need to. Add the hot stock, stir, and bring the whole thing to a slow boil once again.

The hard work is done. Turn down the heat to maintain a simmer and cook, uncovered, for 4 to 5 hours. It may take a little fiddling, but adjust the heat to the precise point that just a bubble or two rises slowly, over and over. Stir every 20 to 30 minutes, especially along the sides and bottom, and add a little more stock or water if it seems to be too thick. In basic terms, you are letting time and a little heat do their magic. At the very end, taste the sauce and adjust the seasoning. Depending on many factors, it may need some salt. And add some pepper.

If you are going to use some of the Bolognese sauce immediately, then heat a big pot of water, salt it well, and add the pasta. Stir so it doesn't stick and cook until it is nearly done, 1 minute less than the package directions.

Add 1 cup of the sauce to a medium sauté pan and let it heat until softly bubbling. If need be, add a little of the pasta water to loosen the sauce.

When the pasta is nearly done, drain it quickly and add it, still a little wet, to the sauté pan and stir to bring sauce and pasta together. (If you are serving the pasta as a main course, increase the sauce to 3 cups and the pasta to at least 1 pound. That should be enough for four people.)

Cook only for a minute or so, and then turn the heat off. Add a handful of grated Parmesan, a little salt and fresh ground pepper, and some parsley. When you serve each plate, add a little more grated cheese and parsley to the top.

NOTE: I make my Bolognese sauce with red or white wine. I will use white wine in the summer and red wine in the winter. But more often, it is simply a case of having ½ cup (120 ml) of one or the other left over and using that.

Spaghetti and Dungeness Crab

1 (28-ounce/785-g) can San
   Marzano tomatoes, crushed

6 tablespoons (¾ stick/85 g)
   good cold, unsalted butter

1 medium yellow onion, peeled
   but root and top kept on to
   hold it together, and halved

Sea salt and fresh ground black
   pepper

2 fresh 1- to 1½-pound
   (455- to 680-g) Dungeness
   crabs, steamed and gutted
   but not shelled

½ pound (225 g) good-quality
   dried spaghetti

½ cup (25 g) mixed chopped
   fresh flat-leaf parsley and basil

SERVES 4 TO 6

**I will make this dish whenever I can get fresh crab. The first task is
to make the sauce. It stems from a famous Marcella Hazan recipe:
tomatoes, onion, and butter. There is a sweetness to Dungeness crab,
and the butter and onion are perfect for that sweetness.**

Heat a saucepan over medium heat for a minute. Add the crushed
tomatoes, butter, and onion and bring to a low boil. Stir, add some salt
and pepper, and let the mixture bubble gently for 30 to 40 minutes. Stir
every 10 minutes or so.

Break the crab in half, holding each side, and rinse under cold water.
Then, starting at the back legs and holding a thumb at their joint, break
each leg, pulling toward the back. Do the same with each claw. This
should get you the very tasty meat from that last joint of each leg.

Rinse the legs and, using a crab cracker, break off that last joint and put
whatever meat you gather into a clean, small bowl. Do this for all the
legs. For the claws, also take off the last joint and do some preliminary
cracking of the shells. Pick over the meat, discarding any pieces of shell.

Let the legs sit in a colander to drain, but do not refrigerate them.
Gently break the two halves of the body in half again. You cannot use
too much force or the cell structure, which is holding the crabmeat, will
be crushed. Pick out any loose pieces of body walls.

Bring a big pot of water to a boil. Add a good pinch of salt. When the
sauce has thickened a little and begun to separate into a show of fat on
the surface, then it is time to add the pasta to the boiling water.

Cook the pasta for 9 to 10 minutes—taste it at 9. When it has just
stopped being firm, pull it quickly from the water and lay it, still slightly
dripping, into the sauce and stir it to combine. The starch from the
pasta should thicken the tomato sauce even further.

Moving quickly, use a strainer to lower the cracked crab pieces into the
pasta water. Give a shake and pull the strainer out and lay the crab over
the pasta and tomato sauce.

Add some salt and pepper and the parsley-basil mixture. Stir slightly to
mix. Transfer to a hot serving bowl, making sure that the crab pieces
are a fair mix of legs and body. Add the rest of the parsley-basil and any
loose crab meat and serve immediately.

Your Own Tomato Sauce

1 (28-ounce/785-g) can San
 Marzano tomatoes

¼ cup (60 ml) extra-virgin
 olive oil

3 garlic cloves, minced

Pinch of red pepper flakes

½ cup (20 g) loosely packed
 fresh basil, then chopped or
 torn into small pieces

Sea salt and fresh ground black
 pepper

MAKES 1½ CUPS (360 ML)

**In the long-term interest of saluting the taste and standard of
the tomato, here is a very simple recipe for tomato sauce. If you
are making a tomato sauce, then you want to go a few lengths to
make it a good sauce. Do not scrimp on the finish—only use freshly
grated true Parmesan. If you are adding it to pasta, have the pasta
on course to be ready right at the moment when you finish the
sauce. Mix them together, always saving a little hot pasta water
to thin the sauce if necessary.**

Pour the tomatoes and their juices into a stainless-steel bowl. With
clean hands, lightly crush the tomatoes.

Heat a saucepan over medium heat. Add the olive oil and garlic and cook
for 2 minutes only, being careful not to brown the garlic at all. Stir and add
the red pepper flakes, crushed tomatoes, half the basil, and some salt and
black pepper. Stir and stay with it. When it comes to a boil, turn the heat
down immediately to maintain a very slow, gentle simmer.

Simmer for 40 minutes, stirring every 6 minutes or so. Keep the simmer
slow and steady and add a little water if the sauce seems to be drying
out. When you stir, be careful to reach to the bottom of the pan to
bring up the thicker base.

After 40 minutes, the sauce will be done, thickened and rich. Remove
the pan from the heat. Taste and adjust the seasoning, and add the rest
of the basil before serving. You can freeze the sauce in airtight jars—it
will keep for weeks.

A Modern Fish Stew

2 to 3 pounds (910 g to 1.4 kg)
mixed fresh fish fillets, such as
monkfish, cod, halibut, snapper

1 pound (455 g) small clams (you
only need 6 to 8, so choose
the best ones)

1 pound (455 g) mussels (6 to
8 total)

½ pound (225 g) large shrimp in
the shell (6 to 8)

½ pound (225 g) bay scallops

¾ cup (180 ml) extra-virgin
olive oil

1 medium yellow or red onion,
finely chopped

6 garlic cloves: 4 coarsely
chopped, 2 halved

½ teaspoon red pepper flakes

2 medium carrots, finely chopped

Sea salt and fresh ground black
pepper

1 cup (50 g) chopped fresh flat-
leaf parsley

¾ cup (180 ml) dry white wine

1½ pounds (680 g) fresh
tomatoes, peeled and seeded,
or 1 (28-ounce/785-g) can San
Marzano tomatoes

1 bay leaf

8–10 slices white country bread,
sliced on a bias

SERVES 4 TO 6

If there is a place between bouillabaisse and paella, between Italian *cacciucco* and New England clam chowder, it is this fish stew. It is too young to have much of a reputation, but that means you are part of what it shall become. It is a modest proposal—a simple, fresh fish stew.

I use fillets of cod as the base and then select from monkfish, snapper, and halibut, for they are generally available and fresh. You need them to be of the best quality.

Rinse the fish fillets, skin them, and dry them. Cut them into 1-inch (2.5-cm) pieces. Put the pieces of each in separate small bowls and set aside.

Rinse the clams, mussels, shrimp, and scallops. Scrub the clams, debeard the mussels, peel and devein the shrimp, and pat the scallops partly dry.

Preheat the broiler.

Heat a heavy-bottomed, high-sided pan over medium heat for a minute. Add ¼ cup (60 ml) of the olive oil and heat for 30 seconds. Add the onion, stir, and stay with it so the oil coats the onion and the onion starts to lightly brown. Add the coarsely chopped garlic, red pepper flakes, carrots, and some salt and black pepper. Stir again, and cook for 2 to 3 minutes, being careful not to let the garlic burn. Preheat the broiler.

Stir in half the parsley and then ½ pound (225 g) of the cod (or the firmest fish, if not using cod) and ½ cup (120 ml) of the wine. Cook for 5 minutes to reduce the wine by at least half and give the fish time to break down and merge with the vegetables.

Add the tomatoes, bay leaf, and a sprinkle of salt. Cook, uncovered, for 5 to 7 minutes, making certain nothing sticks or burns.

For the bread, make sure the broiler is up to temperature and that you have a warmed platter to put the slices on. Once the slices are browned or even slightly blackened, pull them out, rub their surfaces with a cut piece of raw garlic, and sprinkle some salt and a couple dribbles of olive oil over their tops. (Alternatively, you can fry the bread in olive oil. Heat ¼ cup/60 ml of the olive oil in a sauté pan over low heat. Add the bread and brown on each side for about 2 minutes, then transfer the slices to a warmed platter, rub with the garlic, and sprinkle with some salt. If you fry the bread, you will use considerably more olive oil.)

Return to the fish stew. Poke and crush the tomatoes with a wooden spoon, if need be, to hurry the process. Give it all a good stir and then carefully add all the remaining fish pieces to the mix. Add a good sprinkle of salt and pepper and let it simmer for a minute.

Add the shrimp, cook for another minute, then add the rest of the shellfish (clams, mussels, and scallops) right on top without stirring. Pour the remaining ¼ cup (60 ml) wine over it all and cover the pan tightly so the shellfish can steam open.

The stew is done when the clams and mussels open. You can pull out the ones that open and put them in a small bowl. After 6 minutes, pull them all out and throw away any shellfish that did not open.

Work quickly and ladle the stew into warmed soup bowls, adding some of the shellfish to each. Sprinkle some parsley, drizzle lightly with olive oil, and finally, tuck a piece of the toasted bread into the corner of each soup. Your fish soup is up and ready.

VARIATIONS: As you get comfortable making the fish stew, there are some important variations to consider. Fennel, for example. Chop a half or whole bulb of fennel and add it to the base with the chopped garlic. It is a very appropriate nod to the Mediterranean fish soup tradition and history.

There is some tradition for adding potatoes to the stew. They will give it body and length, the starch thickening the broth and the potato itself adding heft. For this stew, you should use a Yellow Finn or other thin-skinned potato. Peel about 1 pound (455 g) of potatoes and cut them into ½-inch (12-mm) slices. Lay the slices on top of the tomato base and let them cook with the tomato for 5 minutes more, then add the fish pieces right on the top and gently stir it all together.

I have not included salmon. It is too oily to be used in the regular lineup. But it is a wonderful fish, and I have added it many times to my fish stews, and been pleased to have it there. Use no more than ½ pound (225 g) of salmon and have it be a thicker piece, cut into chunks as you would for a beef stew. Salt the salmon pieces and add them last, with the shrimp, so the salmon is cooked quickly and retains some separateness.

The Last Chicken Noodle Soup Recipe You Will Need

2 bone-in, skin-on organic
chicken breasts, about
¾ pound (340 g) each

Sea salt and fresh ground
black pepper

Extra-virgin olive oil, as needed

1 or 2 sprigs fresh thyme or
rosemary (optional)

7 or 8 cups (1.7 to 2 L)
homemade chicken stock
(page 35)

4 tablespoons (½ stick/60 g)
cold, unsalted butter

2 medium leeks, rinsed well,
white parts finely chopped

½ cup (120 ml) dry white wine,
plus more as needed

1 bunch fresh flat-leaf parsley,
finely chopped

2 garlic cloves: 1 minced, 1 halved

1 medium yellow onion, halved:
½ finely chopped, ½ thinly
sliced into rings

½ pound (225 g) chanterelles
or hedgehog mushrooms,
cleaned and chopped into
finger-size pieces

½ pound (225 g) good-quality
dried egg fettuccine
(see Note on page 230)

½ cup (50 g) freshly grated
Parmigiano-Reggiano cheese

6 slices crusty white farmhouse
bread

SERVES 4

I love chicken noodle soup. I loved it in cans as a kid. I loved it in the school lunch line, from a thermos while hiking in the mountains, and in England for lunch on a construction site.

I rarely made it myself. I could not imagine how to approach it. But now I have it—I have it because I have fussed for years with cooking chicken, with cooking fresh mushrooms, with making stock, with gathering multiple ingredients, with sweating onions, with choosing pastas. I have it because a good chicken noodle soup brings an order and elegance to all its parts and that alone made it interesting to me. Done correctly, it is an evening meal in and of itself, and a lunch to be anticipated. I make it with a nod to England, a nod to Tuscany, a nod to Vietnam, and a nod to the woods and trails of Whidbey Island in the fall.

It is not difficult, but it has parts and pieces and choreography, so stay close. You must of course begin with good chicken stock. You can make the stock yourself (see page 35). That is best, and it is in truth quite easy, save for the cleanup. Or you can buy it freshly made, even frozen. That is second best. Or you can buy it off the shelf, which will work in a pinch but has some kinship to bringing Wisconsin Parmesan to Italy. Use what you can get—the important thing is to make the soup.

At our best, we make the soup to serve in a sequence of meals. We may roast a chicken or two over the weekend, making stock from the bones that are left, and then serve the noodle soup on whatever night seems most suited. If need be, we freeze the extra stock until we know what night is best for the soup. Most of the time we buy extra chicken breasts to add to the soup, but there have been times we simply used the leftover meat from the roasted chicken (see page 209).

Good stock is crucial, but good chicken is even more essential. The meat is quick roasted and added to the soup at the very end—you will taste it clearly. Find a source for fresh organic chicken.

This may seem a hefty recipe, but it is simply specific. Each time that you make it, it will go more quickly.

Preheat the oven to 400°F (205°C).

Pull the chicken breasts from the fridge and let them come to room temperature. Pat them dry with paper towels, then transfer them to a stainless-steel bowl and season well with salt and pepper, rubbing the seasoning into and a little under the skin. Drizzle a little olive oil over them and rub it over all sides of the breasts. If you have a little thyme or rosemary on the counter, you can lay a sprig or two on top. Let the chicken sit out for 20 minutes with a glass plate over the bowl.

Heat a low-sided baking dish or ovenproof sauté pan for a minute in the oven. Put the chicken in the pan, skin side down, and scrape any seasoning and olive oil from the bowl onto the bony upside. Put the pan in the oven and note the time. The chicken should be done in about 45 minutes. After 15 minutes, open the door and carefully turn the chicken breasts over, so they are skin side up. Try to not tear the skin—a thin spatula can help with this. Do not open the door again until you believe they are done cooking.

Meanwhile, in a medium pot, bring the stock to a simmer.

Heat a 4- or 5-quart (3.8- to 4.7-L) French oven or heavy stainless-steel casserole over medium heat for a minute. Add a drizzle of olive oil and 2 tablespoons of the butter. When it has melted, add the leeks and stir to combine. You are softening the leeks, not browning them, but not trying to lull them to sleep, either.

After 10 minutes, add half the wine—it should sizzle a little. Cook until it has nearly evaporated. Add 5 cups (1.2 L) of the stock and bring it to a soft boil. Taste and adjust the seasoning. Some stocks are very salty; some not at all. You need to get it just right. Add as much salt and fresh pepper as it seems to need. The truth is, a good chicken soup is, at its heart, a little salty. Throw in a small handful of the parsley. Let the soup softly boil.

If you can smell the chicken, and it has been nearly 45 minutes, check it. It should be crispy, sticking slightly to the pan, and firmed up. It should register 160 to 165°F (70 to 75°C) on a meat thermometer. Transfer the chicken to a warmed plate.

To make gravy, pour off most of the liquid fat in the pan. Set the roasting pan on the stovetop over low heat. Add a ladle of the stock, scrape up any browned bits stuck to the bottom of the pan, and let it all bubble for 3 to 4 minutes, adding more stock if need be.

After 10 minutes or so, add a tablespoon of wine and a pinch of the minced garlic. A minute later, add 1 tablespoon of the butter and stir. It should thicken a bit and you should have about ½ cup (120 ml) of gravy. Add some salt, pepper, and parsley. I usually pour it into a glass coffee cup or bowl and set it near the cooking soup to stay warm. If the gravy is too thick, thin it with a little stock.

Heat an 8- or 10-inch (20- or 25-cm) sauté pan over medium heat for a minute. Add a little olive oil and 1 tablespoon of the butter. When the butter has melted, add the chopped onion and stir. A minute or so later, add the onion rings and the mushrooms; stir and season with salt and pepper. Add a little parsley and get it all working together. When the mushrooms seem to stick to the pan a bit, add half a ladle of the stock (if they do not stick a little, the heat is too low). This is all happening in a kind of 2-4-2 time: 2 minutes to start the onions, 4 to cook the mushrooms, 2 to set the sauce (a handy format to keep in mind when cooking fresh mushrooms). Before the sauce sets up, add a sip of the wine and the remaining minced garlic; stir and consider if it might need a touch more stock. Taste the mushrooms for seasoning. They should be a little firm but cooked through. Take the pan off the heat.

Add the pasta to the soup, stir well, and stay close to it. You do not want it to overcook.

Preheat the broiler.

Assemble the soup: For each serving, ladle in enough broth to come three-quarters of the way up the sides of a warmed bowl. Add 1 tablespoon of the mushrooms. With tongs, add some pasta. Move somewhat quickly, because you want the soup hot enough to melt some of the Parmesan. Slice the chicken, keeping a little skin attached, and lay it into the pasta and broth. Add Parmesan and perhaps a little salt.

Add the remaining mushrooms on top, a good serving-spoon's worth for each bowl. Add a teaspoon of the gravy, a good sprinkling of parsley, a few grinds of pepper, and, for the very end, a slight spoonful of the soup broth itself, to glisten.

The bread needs to be broiled quickly, until there is the slightest char on each side (leftover bread is in some ways best for this). Then lay the pieces on a warm plate. Rub them with the halved garlic cloves for a second. Quickly sprinkle them with salt and pepper and parsley and a drizzle of good olive oil and get it to the soup eaters. If you have been timely and nimble, then serve it on the plate beside the soup. If the bread is good and you take the moments to char it, to rub it, to season it, and oil it, then it is hard to make enough bread.

NOTE: You must decide or learn what pasta to add to your soup. We use an egg pasta from Rustichella d'Abruzzo, a very thin, flat fettuccine, which cooks in 4 minutes. We have also used their spaghetti, which cooks in 12 minutes, and an orecchiette that takes 15 minutes. They each have advantages, as do true fresh pastas that might need only 2 minutes. We choose the fettuccine for how it lies flat in the liquid; it does not try to jump loose as you eat and seems to hold its form well the next day.

What you must keep in mind is the time needed to cook the pasta, whichever type you are using. You should always slightly undercook pasta in a soup. It will still be in hot liquid, even after the soup is off the heat.

As to quantity, you must take into account how much it will swell and how much room it will take up. I want the pasta, but I also want the soup—I want to see the broth. As a rule, I always try to use less, not more. You can, if unsure, keep a pan of salted water at a low boil on the side and cook pasta there as needed, then transfer it to the soup.

If you are using a pasta that takes more than 10 minutes to cook, I suggest you add the pasta to the stock as you begin to cook the mushrooms. If it is a quick-cooking fresh pasta, then you can add it just as they are nearly done. The mushrooms are best if they are used within minutes of being cooked, rather than letting them get a bit limp in their own sauce.

TOOLBOX
Five Essential Skills

This is a "how-to" toolbox, built to keep a few details easily handy. As you get familiar with cooking beans or rice, couscous, quinoa, or lentils, you will move on to tackling more complications to each dish.

But I still find there are days that I need to review just how I want to get the rice cooked. That is what a toolbox is for—to lean on the order of things.

How to Cook Beans

1 cup (185 g) dried cranberry
(Borlotti) or cannellini beans

1 bay leaf

2 garlic cloves, crushed

MAKES 2 CUPS (ABOUT 350 G)

Time and history are not, of course, the only wisdom, but there is a tradition for soaking dried beans and that is how I do it. I know that this modern life has few things that need soaking and few things that need priming or curing or leaving overnight, but I gladly make an exception for beans. I am proud to see them soaking, up there on the counter. In a way, cooking beans is like actually reading a book: You have to plan for it.

Soak the beans, covered and unrefrigerated, in a bowl with ample cold water for 12 to 24 hours (change the water a couple of times if you can). Drain and rinse well.

Transfer the beans to a large pot and add water to cover by 3 inches (7.5 cm) or so. Add the bay leaf and garlic and bring the water to a boil. Do not cover the pot and do not salt the water.

Turn the heat down a little—it should cook at a gentle roll—and cook the beans until they have softened but are not mushy, about 45 minutes (the exact time will depend on the age of the beans). Make sure to stir every 15 minutes or so, to keep the beans moving. If you need to add more liquid, make sure the water is hot so that you maintain a boil.

Turn off the heat and let the beans cool in the liquid. Discard the bay leaf. Once cooled, decant the beans and their cooking liquid into a glass container with a tight lid and refrigerate for 4 to 5 days.

How to Cook Rice

I used to cook rice by boiling the grains in salted water and then draining them. Or by steaming the rice in a covered pan until the water has evaporated. Or by making risotto. But I have been diverted by the rice cooking of Tessa Kiros in her cookbook *Falling Cloudberries*. She cooks with instincts from Greece and Peru, from Finland and Tuscany, and it all loosens the script. These are adapted from her recipes.

A BASIC RICE

MAKES 1½ CUPS (260 G)

2 tablespoons extra-virgin olive oil

1 garlic clove

1 cup (180 g) basmati rice

Sea salt

This is now my preferred method for cooking rice—it adds a flavor I love.

The garlic softens into the rice and the slight toasting of the grains distinguishes them. The basmati rice will keep well in the refrigerator; it is long and lean. I will sometimes make a single cup of rice when using the rice for tortillas or pita bread. It is at its best moments after cooking.

Heat a small saucepan over medium heat. Add 1 tablespoon of the olive oil and the garlic. Let the garlic heat for a minute, then add the rice and a pinch of salt, and toast the rice in the oil for 2 minutes, stirring to prevent burning.

Add water to cover the rice by 1 inch (2.5 cm)—it should sizzle for a moment when it hits the pan. Stir and let the heat cook off much of the liquid. When you see four or five holes in the rice, then stir once more, add the remaining 1 tablespoon olive oil, turn the heat down a bit, and put a lid on the pan. The rice will be fully cooked in 10 minutes more. Let it rest for a couple of minutes and then fluff it with a fork before serving.

RICE COOKED WITH LEMON AND BUTTER

SERVES 4

2 tablespoons cold, unsalted butter, plus more as needed

3-inch (7.5-cm) strip lemon peel, no pith

1 tablespoon sea salt

2 cups (360 g) basmati rice, rinsed well in cold water

This is rice to accompany bolder things—roasted chicken, beef with herbs, fish that has been baked with oregano, or vegetables like asparagus and peas—that love the reference to lemon and butter.

In a medium saucepan, combine 4 cups (960 ml) water, the butter, lemon peel, and salt. Bring to a boil, then add the rice; stir and lower the heat to maintain a simmer. Cook, uncovered, for 14 minutes, then cover the pan for a minute.

Fluff the rice with a fork, taste for salt, and add perhaps another tablespoon of cold butter.

How to Cook Lentils (and Lentil Soup)

1 ½ cups (300 g) lentils, preferably le Puy

3 cups (720 ml) homemade chicken stock (page 35; if making soup, you will need 5 to 6 cups/1.2 to 1.4 L)

2 tablespoons extra-virgin olive oil, plus more for drizzling

1 medium yellow onion, finely chopped

1 carrot, finely chopped

1 celery stalk, finely chopped

1 bay leaf

1 garlic clove, peeled

1 sprig fresh sage

Sea salt

2 tablespoons cold, unsalted butter

½ cup (50 g) freshly grated Parmigiano-Reggiano cheese

Fresh ground pepper

MAKES 2 TO 3 CUPS (310 TO 470 G); ENOUGH SOUP TO SERVE 4

Lentils are the best host. You should experiment with different lentil varieties; they are each quite particular, in taste and texture and color. This is a basic technique for cooking any of them. Take this recipe just a few steps further and you can make a basic lentil soup instead. You can make this a day or two before you need it (for me, it is usually made on Sunday). Then later in the week, you can dress it up with the help of rice, sausage, pasta, or broccoli rabe, putting it to use in the recipes on pages 163–172. Or you could also add chopped parsley and a little lemon juice and grated lemon zest. Or stir in small leaves of arugula and a little feta cheese.

Soak the lentils in cold water for 10 minutes. In a medium pot, bring the stock to a simmer.

In the meantime, heat a soup pan over medium heat. Add the olive oil, onion, carrot, and celery, and cook until softened.

Drain the lentils and add them to the pan. Add the bay leaf, garlic, and sage and stir well to combine. After 5 minutes, as the lentils begin to stick to the pan, add enough stock to cover the lentils by about 1 inch (2.5 cm) and turn the heat down a little. Let the lentils simmer, uncovered, for 35 to 40 minutes. If they get too dry, add a little more stock. Stir every 5 minutes or so.

The lentils are done when they are soft, but not mushy. Remove and discard the bay leaf and the sage. Taste and adjust the seasoning—it will need salt, as none was added beforehand. Add the butter, cheese, and some pepper. Stir to combine. Your lentils are ready to be put to use. They can be stored in airtight containers for up to a week.

However, should you want to make the lentils into a soup, then wait to add the butter and cheese.

Scoop out two-thirds of the lentils and run them through a food mill or food processor and return them to the pan. With the heat on medium-low, slowly add the larger amount of the stock, stirring well. The soup should thicken and set a little. Now you must taste and adjust the seasoning.

Stir the grated Parmesan into the soup with the butter, as you would for a risotto. Serve it hot and with a thin line of olive oil on the surface.

How to Cook Couscous

1 teaspoon salt

1 tablespoon extra-virgin olive oil

1 cup (195 g) couscous, wheat or whole wheat

MAKES 3 CUPS (540 G)

The couscous in today's supermarket is precooked. It does not need or want to be boiled any further—it needs simply to be revived in water that has boiled.

Bring 1½ cups (360 ml) of water to a boil. Add the salt and the olive oil, and then the couscous. Turn off the heat, stir once, and cover. The couscous is ready in 8 minutes. Fluff it well with a fork.

Store it in an airtight container in the refrigerator—it will be fine for 2 to 3 days.

VARIATION: Use chicken stock or vegetable stock (see pages 35–36) instead of water. It will add a flavor to the couscous.

How to Cook Quinoa

1 tablespoon extra-virgin olive oil

1 cup (170 g) quinoa, rinsed well

1 teaspoon salt

MAKES 2½ TO 3 CUPS (500 TO 600 G)

You must always rinse quinoa. There is a natural coating on each seed that can create a bitter taste when cooked—a careful rinse will wash the coating away. (Much of the quinoa sold today has already been rinsed, but there is no harm to refreshing the seed.)

Heat a saucepan on medium heat and add the olive oil. After a moment, add the quinoa and salt. Let that toast for a minute and then add 2 cups (480 ml) of water and stir. When the contents come to a rolling boil, turn the heat down to low, stir once, and cover the pan.

The temperature should be enough to keep the quinoa at a slow simmer. The quinoa will be done in 15 minutes.

Turn the heat off and let it rest, covered, for 2 minutes. Then fluff it with a fork.

Store it in an airtight container in the refrigerator—it will be fine for 2 to 3 days.

VARIATION: Use chicken or vegetable stock (see pages 35–36), instead of water.

MENUS
Five Ways to a Meal

Obviously, these are not a prescription, nor even a playlist. These five menus, ranging from roughly less complicated to more, are meant to give a sense of what can be linked and partnered, of what can work best together, of what can lead and what can follow.

A menu has only the details of the foods available—it tries to vary weights and colors, acids and proteins, fiber and starch. A menu has intuitions about food, but it has no intuitions about your day. That is your task—to gather the details that will help to construct a menu that fits—and fits the day.

A STRAIGHTFORWARD DINNER

There are days that need a straightforward approach.
When they come, I want to be ready. A good pasta and a salad is
often my plan. And best repair. Be careful to choose dishes that are
themselves straightforward, in detail and in preparation.

A light, sparkling wine such as MORPHOS,
from Oyster River Winegrowers in Warren, Maine

ASPARAGUS, GRILLED
(page 81)

CACIO E PEPE (page 188)

GREEN SALAD
with MEYER LEMON DRESSING (page 73)

FROMAGE D'AFFINOIS
served with BUTTER and THIN TOAST

The next day: Should you have extra pasta, the *cacio e pepe* is
wonderful reheated for lunch. You could even add the asparagus.
Refresh the pasta with just a touch of lemon juice, Parmesan,
and perhaps a drizzle of olive oil.

Menu 2

REASONABLY QUICK AND WONDERFUL

If you can do it, stop and get some lamb thigh or a hanger
steak for dinner. They are both quick and wonderful. Whatever the
possibilities, you can set a table with many small variations of this
basic menu—a bit of broccoli, a soft cheese, a few mushrooms, some
rice—and make the sum seem much more than the parts. Your best
allies are the different colors.

A Spanish sparkling wine, such as
VINYES SINGULARS CAVA BRUT NATURE

Something seasonal—ASPARAGUS, TOMATOES,
or MUSHROOMS, by themselves

CHÈVRE sprinkled with CHIVES and CIABATTA

LAMB THIGH or HANGER STEAK (page 203 or 207)

BROCCOLI with GARLIC, OIL, and
HOT PEPPER (page 93)

RICE with EGG, PANCETTA, and PARMESAN
(page 150)

Fresh APPLES, sliced and sprinkled with a little
LEMON JUICE

The next day: Both the lamb and the hanger steak make fine leftovers,
and the rice is always a good companion.

Menu 3

A FRIDAY NIGHT FEAST

I love roasting a chicken on a Friday. It is easy enough to get it
ready for the oven, it takes only minimal attention once it is cooking,
and it does not mind sitting around, even for twenty minutes, while
you do other things. Also, you have all weekend to make a stock
from the carcass and time to use that stock.

GRÜNER VELTLINER,
Austrian, Slovakian, or a new one from Oregon

LENTILS DRESSED with CROUTONS
and FRESH PARMESAN (page 164)

ROASTED CHICKEN (page 209)
with SAUTÉED CHANTERELLES, if available

COUSCOUS to CARRY in the SQUASH (page 179)

BROCCOLI FAIR with BUTTER and
PARMESAN CHEESE (page 94) or the CARROTS
ROASTED with HERBS (page 107), or both

APPLESAUCE (page 69) and a PEAR with
PARMIGIANO-REGGIANO

A sip of AVERNA (see page 39), to celebrate the meal

The next day: Should you have any leftovers, combine them.
The lentils and couscous are great together, and the squash will mix
easily with carrots or broccoli.

A BUOYANT PRESENTATION

The pita with cilantro salsa and yogurt makes a light, fresh start to the dinner. The pasta—with crab legs pointing every which way, the tomato sauce, and scattered parsley—makes a buoyant presentation as the main attraction. Serve the baguette with the pasta—you will need it to sop up the tomato sauce and crab.

A light PILSNER beer or a sparkling chilled
red wine like a LAMBRUSCO

SALSA VERDE (page 25) with PITA and
seasoned YOGURT or GRILLED AVOCADO
(or both together)

SPAGHETTI and DUNGENESS CRAB (page 221)

SAUTÉED SWISS CHARD
(see page 26)

BAGUETTE, heated and sliced, and
good BUTTER with SALT

BUTTER LETTUCE SALAD, ALONE (page 23)

AMARO MONTENEGO, later (see page 39)

The next day: I rarely have any leftovers from this meal. But if you do, make a fresh salad with a vinaigrette dressing and lightly fold in the pasta with crab (shell any crab pieces first).

A PARTICULAR MEAL

I try to set at least one day a week aside for a particular meal—
one that I know will take a little longer, will involve more shopping,
or more attention.

One is fish stew. It is a wonderful concoction, but it does take some
shopping, it does make a mess, and as with any fish, you must stay
right with it. As you put it together, you learn to buy a coarse bread
for toasting, to find a good cold white wine to go with it, and you learn
to make certain you have salad greens for afterward. You need a salad
after fish, particularly a stew that concentrates the fish taste. But avoid
feta or Parmesan, and stick with the fresh greens themselves. A starter
of pickled vegetables would be good company to an Aperol apéritif
(see page 39). They suit the fish stew as well—clean and particular.

APEROL SPRITZ apéritif: 2 parts PROSECCO,
1 part APEROL, a splash of SODA, and a slice of ORANGE,
on the rocks (this drink is always a good lead-in to seafood!)

Drink with meal: Any dry SAUVIGNON BLANC,
or a classic ITALIAN SOAVE

PICKLED CARROTS and PICKLED RED ONIONS
(pages 111 and 119)

A MODERN FISH STEW (page 225) with toasted coarse BREAD

BUT-A-MINUTE ARUGULA SALAD (page 21)
with BUTTER LETTUCE added

A DESSERT of FRESH FRUIT (page 246)

The next day: Rarely is there any fish stew left, but if there should be, toss any shells and refrigerate the stew in a tight container. Scrape any parsley or even bread crumbs into the stew. When you reheat it, do so quickly so you avoid cooking the seafood further. You can add cooked rice, spaghetti, or quinoa to stretch it a little. The pickled carrots and onions, of course, can be kept together but seal them well and refrigerate. Bring them to room temperature before serving again.

A Sweet End to the Meal,
A Dessert of Fresh Fruit

¼ cup sugar, plus 1 tablespoon,
   if desired

1 cup (180 g) fresh fruit, washed,
   peeled, and cut into small bite-
   size pieces

1 pound (450 g) fresh fruit,
   washed, peeled, and cut into
   slightly larger bite-size pieces

Lemon wedges (optional)

SERVES 4

If you should need a dessert, let it be fresh fruit. Present the fruit both cooked and raw for a simple but endlessly adaptable sweet end to a meal. Make this with any combination of fruit that you like: strawberries, raspberries, peaches, blueberries, apples, pears, etc.

Do not wash raspberries—it steals too much of their taste—and plums are another exception—I slice them but do not peel them, preferring the dark color and taste of their skin.

Bring ¼ cup water and ¼ cup of the sugar to a slow, soft boil in a saucepan.

Let it cook for 2 minutes until the sugar is combined and then add the 1 cup (180 g) of small-cut fruit.

Stir the fruit well and let it bubble slightly on medium-low heat for 5 to 10 minutes. You want the fruit to break down and soften—but only half-way. Adjust the time based on the type of fruit. (Obviously a ripe black-berry will need less time than a firm apple.) Keep stirring, adding a touch of water if needed, until you have a thickened sauce and the half-softened pieces of fruit. Take the pan off the heat and let the sauce cool.

Put the 1 pound (450 g) of cut fruit into a ceramic or glass bowl.

Taste a piece. If the fruit is tart, add the remaining tablespoon of sugar and stir to combine. If it is fleshy, as an apple or pear, squeeze a tiny bit of lemon juice over the fruit to hold it from browning.

Now construct and assemble. I use small glass plates or shallow bowls, so everything is quite visible. In simplest form, lay 1 tablespoon of the cooked fruit on the surface and arrange the fresh, uncooked pieces on top of it. Finish with a little bit of the sauce from the cooked fruit.

VARIATIONS: There are a number of toppings that can be added to the fruit to provide texture and nuance. Here are a few ideas.

Whipping cream: Whip the cream, ¼ cup or so, with 1 tablespoon of sugar, and lay that on top of the fruit, and then a touch of cooked fruit sauce.

Mint: Be cautious or the mint will flavor everything. Tiny, thin slivers can be added as a garnish on top of the fruit, or rub apple slices with the leaf itself.

Fresh granola: Use only 1 teaspoon per serving; granola can be a bully. Sprinkle it on top of the fruit and then always lay something over the granola—cream, sauce, or yogurt.

Maple syrup or honey: Use separately, and with similar restraint. Heat them a little, in a double boiler, before using, for then you can drizzle a very thin stream on top and not overwhelm the fruit.

Semi-sweet chocolate: Use a fine grater and true chocolate and apply it in a dusting of no weight. The fruit will find the chocolate, especially the strawberries and raspberries.

Meringues: Crumble a meringue onto the fruit, both for texture and surprise.

Greek yogurt: Denser than cream, it makes a lovely parfait center. Lay the cooked fruit below, some yogurt and raw fruit folded together, and sauce on top. Finish with a tiny drizzle of warm honey.

Shelled walnuts: Heat them first in a dry small sauté pan until warm and then break them apart and apply them at the very end, around the edges, only 3 or 4 pieces per serving.

EPILOGUE
Cleaning Up

What did I leave out? Figs and peas, potatoes and eggs, a thousand cheeses, as many grains, and more ...

But *Five Ways to Cook Asparagus* was never meant to touch everything. It was to create a sense of how it might be done, this task and honor of cooking. It was to set up a trail system that could safely lead you all over the world of food and cooking. If you have good equipment, if you understand how things work and what they are meant to do, if you can trust your instincts, then you can go in any direction.

It is a modern world. And cooking is an ancient task. They will forever be integral and at opposition. The task is to steer a course through what is available, what is possible, and what is best. There are many factors deflecting you from such a course, and as many that could be wonderful allies to your task. Cooking is daunting and brave, messy and clear.

The most important detail is you, for you must believe that it matters, that it is vital, and that you can do it. You must believe that there is even some magic to it, that a meal well cooked is a gift and a protection and an honor—and an integral part of the task of each day.

INDEX

ACKNOWLEDGMENTS

I am a lucky man. No matter the course of a day, there are always good meals and plenty of books, and they are both best done by hand. Publishing a book takes many hands.

My publisher, Michael Jacobs, is trying to learn Italian to complete his most honored degree, but he insists on reading whatever I send him. My editor, Laura Dozier, has watered and cleaned and exercised and tutored all of my words and each of my books, until they were ready to stand alone.

Les Canalistes have done all of the photography, as ever, but I believe this is among their best work. (They are like cooking for Bette Davis and Katharine Hepburn—no matter how much fun it is, you are still a little nervous.)

John Gall and his team have again designed the book, and again it is the perfect outfit, as if born with the text.

You must have a grant to write a book—it may be no more than a grant of time or table or paper, but you cannot do it without a grant. The architecture firm Suyama Peterson DeGuchi brought my bookshop into their building when we desperately needed a place— they granted me time and company and confidence.

Many people have helped, with enthusiasms that easily coax the task to write. My particular thanks to my children, Nina and Joe, and to Peter and Danielle, Kim and the Mormon twins, Ian and Maret, Nico and Cam, Michael Easton, Karel Cipra, Matt Dillon, Gordon Walker, Rick Sundberg, Jack and Colleen, Bart and Kristin, Peter and Sally Bohlin, Ray Calabro, the Maritz family, all my crew at the shop, all the tasters of Whidbey Island, and my sisters, Sue and Pam.

Many thanks to the family from Alabama that marched into the shop, especially the son for declaring, "That is the only cookbook she uses—unless you write another."

And to my wife, whose watercolor drawings set a perfect dress code for this new book, all my love.

Cook with and use *Five Ways* however seems best for you—it is well-built and should hold up well to tastes and tasks.

ACKNOWLEDGMENTS

I am a lucky man. No matter the course of a day, there are always good meals and plenty of books, and they are both best done by hand. Publishing a book takes many hands.

My publisher, Michael Jacobs, is trying to learn Italian to complete his most honored degree, but he insists on reading whatever I send him. My editor, Laura Dozier, has watered and cleaned and exercised and tutored all of my words and each of my books, until they were ready to stand alone.

Les Canalistes have done all of the photography, as ever, but I believe this is among their best work. (They are like cooking for Bette Davis and Katharine Hepburn—no matter how much fun it is, you are still a little nervous.)

John Gall and his team have again designed the book, and again it is the perfect outfit, as if born with the text.

You must have a grant to write a book—it may be no more than a grant of time or table or paper, but you cannot do it without a grant. The architecture firm Suyama Peterson DeGuchi brought my bookshop into their building when we desperately needed a place—they granted me time and company and confidence.

Many people have helped, with enthusiasms that easily coax the task to write. My particular thanks to my children, Nina and Joe, and to Peter and Danielle, Kim and the Mormon twins, Ian and Maret, Nico and Cam, Michael Easton, Karel Cipra, Matt Dillon, Gordon Walker, Rick Sundberg, Jack and Colleen, Bart and Kristin, Peter and Sally Bohlin, Ray Calabro, the Maritz family, all my crew at the shop, all the tasters of Whidbey Island, and my sisters, Sue and Pam.

Many thanks to the family from Alabama that marched into the shop, especially the son for declaring, "That is the only cookbook she uses—unless you write another."

And to my wife, whose watercolor drawings set a perfect dress code for this new book, all my love.

Cook with and use *Five Ways* however seems best for you—it is well-built and should hold up well to tastes and tasks.

Editor: Laura Dozier
Designers: John Gall and Najeebah Al-Ghadban
Production Manager: Denise LaCongo

Library of Congress Control Number: 2016941985

ISBN: 978-1-4197-2393-3

Text © 2017 Peter Miller
Photography © 2017 Hirsheimer & Hamilton

Abrams books are available at special discounts when
purchased in quantity for premiums and promotions as
well as fundraising or educational use. Special editions
can also be created to specification. For details, contact
specialsales@abramsbooks.com or the address below.

ABRAMS
The Art of Books

115 West 18th Street
New York, NY 10011
www.abramsbooks.com